The Hazel Boyz
The Trails of Four Innocent Men

Authored By:
Deon Patrick
Daniel Taylor
Lewis Gardner
Paul Phillips

The Hazel Boyz : The Trails of Four Innocent Men

Copyright © 2024 by Deon Patrick, Daniel Taylor, Lewis Gardner, Paul Phillips

Get It Done Publishing, LLC. Atlanta, GA

Printed in the United States of America

Paperback ISBN: 978-1-952561-40-5

ePub: 978-1-952561-39-9

All rights reserved. No part of this book may be used or reproduced, stored in a retrieval system, or transmitted in any form or in any manner whatsoever without written permission except in the case of brief quotations embodied in critical articles or reviews.

Acknowledgments

In loving memory of Joseph Brown and all the fallen souls who lost their lives while trying to prove their innocence, this dedication honors those who never made it home. Their struggles against wrongful conviction remain etched in our hearts, a reminder of the injustice they endured. For those still alive but denied the chance to reclaim their freedom, this is a tribute to their resilience, their fight, and the hope that justice will one day prevail. May their spirits inspire us to continue the battle for truth, fairness, and exoneration.

First of all, I would like to thank my mother, Verdis Ruth Patrick, for bringing me into this world and being the best mother a son could ever ask for. It may not have seemed like it, but I was listening when you spoke. As I sit here today, those 16 short years I had with you seem ever so fleeting, yet you instilled values in me that have lasted a lifetime. Your drive to provide my brother and I with a stable life pushes me every day. Watching you get up every day, even when you may not have felt like it, motivates me to be a better man. I hope you are proud of the man I've become, as you will forever live vicariously through me.

I'd also like to thank my grandmothers, Daisy Mae Pratcher and Lenora Clinton. You two put that fight in me and showed me how to stand up for myself when facing adversity. You will forever be loved and remembered.

To my children, Deon Jabari Lockhart and Debra Denette Verdis Kennedy, thank you for allowing me to make mistakes in life and for continuing to love me unconditionally. You two motivate me every day because I know I wasn't a great father, but you've helped me become a better grandfather. Which brings me to my babies, Kamauriana, Marvel, Marlo, and Miracle: Your PaPa loves you so much, and you drive me to create something better in life for y'all. Life has definitely been challenging, yet we are survivors, and we're going to see it through.

I'd also like to thank Mrs. Kenyatta Nicole Patrick for motivating me to write this book and for putting up with a lot of the things I deal with on a daily basis. I'd like to thank Zyria Prater, Mikayla Ezell, and Ernestine Vaughn for allowing me to be a part of their family.

Last but definitely not least, I'd like to thank all the true warriors that came to our aid in this situation: Starting with Steve Mills and Maurice Possley from the Chicago Tribune. I'd also like to thank Northwestern's Center for Wrongful Conviction, most notably Karen Daniel and Rob Warden, among others. My attorneys, Nicole Auerbach and Stuart Chanen, have become my family and will forever be a part of my life. These two have impacted my life in so many ways and continue to do so —they've also influenced how I see life and how I move in life. To anyone I may have forgotten, I want to thank all my true family and friends.

Everyone, stay blessed!

— Deon Patrick

I would like to thank my Lord and Savior, Jesus Christ, who sustained me through everything I had to endure. I also want to express my gratitude to Daniel and Deon's teams and lawyers for making everything possible for each and every one of us. A special thanks to my lawyers at the People's Law Office, Flint Taylor and John Stainthorp, for believing in us enough to pursue our innocence.

I want to give heartfelt thanks to my father, Paul Baker, who is no longer with us, and his wife, Sebrina Baker. I also want to acknowledge my uncles Norman and his wife Terenda, Mike and his wife Deb, and Chamberlin and his wife Kim. I am deeply grateful to my cousins Bradley, Chanel, Lil Mike, Chamberlin, Taylor, Sydney, and Julian, as well as Jonique and her family. My mother, Andrea Phillips, and my brothers Dion, Terrence, and Trenton have been my rock. I also want to thank Shay Jefferson and her family for believing in me. This is my circle of family who has always had my back, showing me love and support through everything I've been through. I truly thank God for each and every one of them.

You can be strong by yourself, but you are even stronger with loving and supportive people around you. If I have missed anyone, I sincerely apologize. Lastly, thank you to Berry Dynamic for making everything happen, for allowing us to share our story, and for taking the time to be part of this journey with us.

In loving memory, I also want to acknowledge my grandmother, Lillie K., who passed away in 2022.

— Paul Phillips

I'd like to thank John Stainthorp and Flint Taylor of the People's Law Office for pursuing this. My wife, for always standing by my side. I want to thank my mother-in-law for helping me through the rough times, and Deon and Daniel for really fighting to see it through. Without their efforts, I don't think I would have ever made it—I don't know about Paul and the others, but I wouldn't have. I also want to thank the newspaper reporter Steven Mills and his team for believing in us and putting the story out there. Thank you Berry Dynamic for all you've done.

— Lewis Gardner

I would like to express my deepest gratitude to Karen Daniel, Judith Royal, Steve Mills, Maurice Possley, David Owens, Donna Finch and

Locke Bowman. Their relentless dedication, expertise, and unwavering belief in my innocence were instrumental in proving the truth and ultimately securing my exoneration. I'd also like to send a deep thank you and appreciation to My Mom for her perseverance and belief in me, may you rest in peace I Love You Dearly. Each of you played a critical role in restoring my freedom and faith in justice. Your support gave me strength when I needed it most, and I will forever be thankful for your commitment to my case and the fight for justice. Thank you from the bottom of my heart.

— Daniel Taylor

On behalf of us all, we wish to extend our deepest gratitude to Ciara Suesberry of Berry Dynamic Agency, whose expertise and unwavering dedication were integral to the creation of this book. Her talent and commitment are imprinted on every chapter, and her efforts have been invaluable in bringing this story to life.

Contents

Introduction	9
1. The Hardship And Hustle Of Deon Patrick	11
2. The Fractured Future Of Paul Phillips	17
3. The Unfolding Nightmare Of Daniel Taylor	24
4. The Relentless Sacrifices Of Lewis Gardner	27
5. The Frame-Up	30
6. The Round Up	34
7. Say This, Sign Here	38
8. Conspired Confessions	48
9. The Courtroom Conspiracy	65
10. Reality Sets In	72
11. A Break In The Clouds	89
12. When The Truth Is All You Have	98
13. A Ray of Light in the Darkness	115
14. The Roller Coaster	125
15. The Crushing Weight of Denial	131
16. The Tide Turns	137
17. Flickers Of Possibility	143
18. Still The Voiceless	151
19. A Lifeline From The Press	157
20. Counting Down The Days To Half-Time	162
21. When Hope Got Tricky	167
22. A Year Of Transition In Stark Darkness	172
23. The State's Reluctance To Acknowledge Truth	182
24. The Confession That Changed Everything	188
25. A Long-Awaited Freedom	192
26. Unshackled Yet Scarred; Life After Injustice	198
27. Healing Through Words	214
28. Resources	216

Introduction

Based on a True Story: The Trials of Four Innocent Men

In the early 1990s, the inner-city of Chicago was a landscape fraught with tension, marked by the infamous reign of the Chicago Police Department. This era, steeped in corruption, torture, false confessions, and mental abuse, saw the lives of countless African-American young men shattered under the weight of systemic injustice. Amidst this backdrop, four young men found themselves ensnared in a harrowing experience that would define their lives.

This is their story—a deep dive into the dark recesses of police interrogation rooms, hidden away from the public eye. In these grim chambers, the relentless drive of overzealous detectives overshadowed the pursuit of truth. Their mission was singular and clear: "Closing This Case After Their Days Off."

Meet Lewis Gardner, Daniel Taylor, Paul Phillips, and Deon Patrick. Their upbringings varied, each marked by unique struggles and dreams, yet they converged on a singular, devastating path. Accused of heinous

Introduction

crimes they did not commit, these four young men were thrust into the unyielding grip of a justice system intent on scapegoating the innocent.

Their journey from childhood to the fateful day of their arrest is a tapestry woven with threads of hope, despair, and resilience. As we unravel their stories, we will witness the profound impact of their wrongful accusations and the brutal reality of their fight for justice. This tale will expose the mechanisms of a corrupt system and the enduring spirit of those who refuse to be broken.

Through their eyes, we will navigate the labyrinth of legal battles, personal sacrifices, and the unyielding quest for vindication. This is not just a story of wrongful imprisonment; it is a testament to the human spirit's capacity to endure and overcome, even in the face of overwhelming odds.

Join us as we embark on this journey, from the innocence of youth to the stark reality of trial, where four lives hang in the balance, fighting for freedom against a backdrop of systemic injustice. This is their story, a story based on true events, a story that demands to be told.

Chapter 1

The Hardship And Hustle Of Deon Patrick

The Transformative Years

Deon Patrick was born on the west side of Chicago, into a family where his parents were married at the time of his birth. He and his brother were raised by their hardworking mother, as their parents separated and ultimately divorced when Deon was just 2 years old. Despite the challenges of being raised by a single mother, Deon's upbringing was filled with love and support from his extensive family network.

Growing up, Deon's mother instilled in him and his brother the importance of education and hard work. She worked long hours at Continental Bank, often leaving early in the morning and not returning until late in the evening. Deon remembers his mother being strict when it came to their schoolwork, always checking their report cards and pushing them to excel academically.

In addition to emphasizing the value of education, Deon's mother also encouraged him to explore his talents and interests. At a young age, Deon began taking piano lessons, following in the footsteps of his brother who played brass instruments. With his mother's support, Deon quickly developed a passion for music and honed his skills on the piano.

However, Deon's childhood was not without its challenges. In the

The Hardship And Hustle Of Deon Patrick

6th grade, their apartment was broken into, prompting his family to make the difficult decision to leave their neighborhood on the west side. They moved to the north side of Chicago, where they experienced a significant culture change from an all-black community to a predominantly Puerto Rican neighborhood.

Despite the gang activity and challenges that came with the move, Deon remained focused on his education and music. With the support of his mother and extended family, he navigated the difficult transition and continued to excel in school and pursue his passion for music.

As Deon entered middle school, he faced new opportunities and challenges in his new neighborhood. The experiences and lessons he learned during this time would shape his future path and set him on a trajectory towards success.

Growing up in the Lincoln Park area of Chicago, Deon Patrick's childhood was filled with memories of the bustling city streets and vibrant community around him. However, it was a block on Agatite Ave that would leave an indelible mark on his life.

Agatite was a block with a lot of apartments, situated in a neighborhood where the cross street was Hazel Street. The building itself was a unique court-shaped building in a U-shape, with five entrances leading into the various hallways. Inside, the hallways were lined with apartments on both sides, creating a sense of community among the residents.

In the early days, Agatite was located in Uptown which was a lively place, with people coming and going at all hours of the day. It was not uncommon to see a lot of activity and traffic in the area, as the residents went about their daily lives. However, beneath the surface of this seemingly bustling neighborhood, there was a darker side to Agatite.

Crime was a prevalent issue in the area, and Deon was no stranger to the challenges that came with living in a neighborhood plagued by violence. Despite the dangers that surrounded him, Deon found solace in the community of Uptown after his mother passed away. It was here that he began to spend more time, seeking comfort and connection in the familiar faces and the shared experiences of his neighbors.

As Deon continued to navigate the ups and downs of life in the Lincoln Park area, Uptown became a place of refuge for him. The block with its unique court-shaped building and bustling hallways provided a sense of belonging and stability in the midst of turmoil.

The passing of Deon Patrick's mother marked a turning point in his life, leaving him to navigate a world filled with challenges and uncertainties. His father, known as June, lived down the street with Deon's grandmother, but their relationship was distant, with Deon never referring to him as Dad. The loss of his mother in 1988, when she was just 38 years old, left a void that could never be filled.

In the days leading up to his mother's death, Deon noticed a change in her health. She had been at home all week, not eating and frequently vomiting. Despite his concerns, Deon never saw his mother seek medical help. Tragically, she passed away the day of his brother returning home from college, leaving Deon and his sibling to grapple with the sudden loss of their mother.

In the wake of her passing, Deon and his brother found themselves inheriting insurance money and receiving their mother's social security checks. However, as the money began to dwindle, Deon turned to selling drugs as a way to make ends meet. The allure of quick money and the weight of responsibilities as a young adult and now a father at the age of 20, pushed Deon into a dangerous world of crime and desperation.

In 1991, at the age of 19, Deon found himself behind bars, convicted of aggravated robbery. As a known gang affiliate, the prison walls seemed to close in on him, separating him from the life he once knew. Upon his release, Deon fell back into old habits, becoming involved in the drug trade once again.

Echoes of a Dark Night

The night had started innocently enough for Deon, a journey from the west side to the north side of the city, a familiar path that carried memories of a childhood marked by loss and upheaval. As he reunited with old friends and navigated the familiar streets, little did he know that the choices made in the haze of that fateful night would lead him down a path of darkness and danger.

Deon's day unfolded in a series of encounters and events that would ultimately converge in a tragic twist of fate. Meeting up with friends, venturing into the projects, and finding himself entangled in a web of conflicts and revelations, Deon's world was a tapestry woven with the threads of crime and the relentless cycle of incarceration that seemed to have him in its grip.

As the night progressed, Deon found himself caught in a whirlwind of events that would forever alter the course of his life. A friend's arrest, a visit to a girlfriend to deliver money obtained through dubious means, and a trip to retrieve stolen speakers all set the stage for the unfolding tragedy that awaited him.

Amidst the backdrop of Monday Night Football and mundane conversations, a sudden revelation shattered the peace of the night. An anonymous death of two strangers, a house raided by police, and the specter of corruption within law enforcement cast a shadow over Deon's world, plunging him into a maelstrom of chaos and uncertainty.

As the authorities closed in, Deon found himself ensnared in a web of suspicion and accusation, his every word scrutinized and his every action weighed against him. With the specter of a gun looming over him and the echoes of a dark night ringing in his ears, Deon was thrust into a world where truth and lies blurred into a murky haze of uncertainty.

As the night wore on, Deon's fate hung in the balance, his past and present colliding in a tumultuous dance of shadows and secrets. With the weight of the world bearing down on him, Deon stood at a crossroads, his future uncertain and his past haunting him like a specter in the night.

Shadows of Deceit

In the heart of the city, a web of deceit unravels, leading to a series of tragic events that will forever alter the lives of those involved. Two people, lost in the grip of addiction, meet a gruesome end, their lives cut short by the tangled web of drugs and desperation.

A man, driven by the need for a fix, rents out his house to fellow addicts, allowing them to indulge in their vices in exchange for a fleeting moment of escape. When a VCR and audio equipment are stolen and sold for drugs, a chain reaction is set in motion, culminating in a brutal act of violence that shakes the very foundations of the community. As the police descend on the scene of the crime, suspicions arise and tensions mount. Handcuffed to the gate, three men from the neighborhood find themselves entangled in a web of lies and betrayal, their fates hanging in the balance as the truth slowly unravels.

It was a night shrouded in darkness, the air heavy with the weight of uncertainty. Daniel, newly released from jail, found himself caught in a web of lies and betrayal that threatened to consume him. As the clock struck 10:30, the echoes of the past collided with the present, setting off a chain reaction of events that would forever alter Deon's life.

Watching the 10 o'clock news from his confinement, Deon witnessed the investigative report of police officers having criminal backgrounds and still being able to work in law enforcement. Coincidently, when the police tried to twist the narrative, claiming the raid happened before the news aired, Deon knew the truth lay buried beneath layers of deceit.

As the police interrogated his friends Daniel and Paul, Deon felt the walls closing in around him. Accusations flew, fingers pointed, and the shadow of the murder hung heavy in the air. Framed for a crime he didn't commit, Deon found himself fighting to prove his innocence in a world where truth was a rare commodity and trust was a fragile thing.

With his every word scrutinized and his every move questioned, Deon must unravel the tangled web of lies that threaten to ensnare him. As the investigation deepens, secrets long buried come to light, casting a harsh spotlight on the darkness that lurks within the shadows of deception. Three men find themselves handcuffed to a gate, caught in the crosshairs of a brutal shooting that sets off a chain reaction of confusion and mistrust. As the police respond to the scene, hidden motives and mistaken identities come to light, shrouding the truth in shadows. Amidst the chaos, Deon and Marshall navigate a treacherous path, their every move scrutinized and their loyalties tested. A dangerous dance of betrayal and deceit unfolds as they grapple with the consequences of their actions.

As the investigation leads to the Phillips house, a veil of secrecy descends, casting a pall over the truth that lies buried within its walls. With police cars lining the streets and tension mounting, Deon and

The Hardship And Hustle Of Deon Patrick

Marshall find themselves ensnared in a web of suspicion and danger. Deon's past collides with the present, forcing him to confront the shadows of his own actions and the dark forces that seek to manipulate him. In a world where loyalty is a rare commodity and trust is a fragile thing, Deon and Marshall must confront the darkness within themselves and the shadows of betrayal that loom ever closer. Chicago was a city where corruption runs deep and justice is a fleeting dream. With his past haunting him and his future uncertain, Deon must confront the forces that seek to destroy him before it's too late.

Chapter 2

The Fractured Future Of Paul Phillips

Shadows of a Summer Day

In the scorching summer of 1985, ten-year-old Paul was a force to be reckoned with in the world of gymnastics, his tumbles and backflips a testament to his skill and agility. Living in the sun-drenched state of mind. Living on North Magnolia at 4455 Magnolia Madras, Paul's days were filled with endless possibilities and carefree exploration.Paul had always been a natural athlete, known for his agility, speed, and dexterity. He was the fastest in his neighborhood, zipping through the streets with the energy and enthusiasm of a young boy who knew no limits. He could tumble and flip with ease, a skill that earned him a spot to try out for the Jesse White Tumbling Team. His acceptance into the team seemed certain, given his impressive abilities and dedication.

One particular day, as Paul and his friends played baseball on the streets of Baldwin, the usual chain barriers that marked the boundaries of their play area were mysteriously absent. As the sun beat down on the streets of North Magnolia, ten-year-old Paul found himself caught in the whirlwind of a fateful baseball game that would forever change the course of his summer. The game progressed with intensity, the children's laughter and cheers filling the air as they played with fervor.

The Fractured Future Of Paul Phillips

Paul, known for his quick movements and daring dashes, found himself at first base, eager to make his way to second. The game rules, with their super caps and strategic placements, added an element of excitement to the day's play. But as Paul attempted his run to second base, the unexpected happened.

A police truck, silent and unnoticed, lurked behind the children's play area, its presence hidden until it was too late. In a moment of confusion and chaos, Paul's back collided with the imposing vehicle, sending him crashing to the ground in a whirl of pain and shock.

As the realization of what had occurred sank in, Paul felt the weight of the truck's tires pressing down on his leg, trapping him in a nightmare of agony. The police truck, oblivious to the chaos it had caused, sped away, leaving Paul injured and bewildered in its wake.

Amidst the chaos, a figure named Troy emerged, with a sense of urgency and care lifted Paul in his arms and carried him home, where Paul's mother awaited, her worry etched deeply on her face. The arrival of the ambulance signaled the seriousness of Paul's injuries, as medical personnel worked swiftly to assess and treat his leg. The pain and confusion of the accident swirled around Paul as he was whisked away to the hospital, his mind reeling with questions and uncertainties.

Paul lay in the hospital bed, his leg encased in a heavy cast that stretched all the way up to his hip. The sterile white walls and the beeping of the machines around him felt like a stark contrast to the carefree summer days he had been enjoying just a short time ago. The sun had been shining brightly when it happened, but now, a cloud of confusion and doubt hung over him, casting a shadow on his thoughts and memories.

He drifted in and out of consciousness, each awakening bringing with it fragments of memories and fleeting whispers of conversations. The details were hazy, like a dream that slips away the moment you try to grasp it. He recalled the sensation of the sun on his skin, the laughter of his friends, and the vibrant colors of summer. But then, there was the accident, a sudden and jarring interruption to his idyllic childhood.

Paul struggled to piece together what had happened. The memories came in disjointed bursts: the sensation of falling, the sharp pain, and the sight of concerned faces hovering above him. He remembered the feeling of the hard ground beneath him and the bright sky above, which seemed so out of place in the midst of his confusion and pain.

He touched the cast on his leg, feeling the rough texture of the plaster. It was a tangible reminder of his injury, a physical manifestation of the trauma he had experienced. He remembered the panic that had gripped him when he first realized he couldn't move his leg, the rush of fear and uncertainty that had flooded his mind.

The hospital room was a blur of doctors and nurses, their voices a constant background hum. Paul could hear snippets of their conversations, words like "fracture," "recovery," and "rehabilitation" filtering through the fog of his mind. He knew that his journey was just beginning, that he would have to summon all his resilience and courage to face the challenges ahead.

Despite the pain and confusion, there was a part of Paul that was determined to understand what had happened. He wanted to know how he had ended up in the hospital, to piece together the events that had led to this moment. He tried to recall the last clear memory he had before everything went dark.

It had been a bright, sunny day. He was with his friends, enjoying the freedom and joy of summer. They had been playing, laughing, and running around without a care in the world. But then something had changed. There was a moment, a split second, when everything shifted. He remembered feeling a strange sense of foreboding, a sense that something was about to go wrong.

The next thing he knew, he was on the ground, pain radiating through his leg. His friends' voices were panicked, their faces pale with fear. Paul had tried to stay conscious, to hold on to the light and warmth of the summer day, but the pain was too much. He had slipped into darkness, the bright sun replaced by the sterile white of the hospital room.

As Paul lay there, the shadows of doubt and suspicion continued to loom large. He knew that the journey ahead would be difficult, that he would need to confront the darkness that lurked beneath the surface of his memories. But he also knew that he had the strength to face whatever came his way.

The whispers of secrets and hidden truths danced at the edges of his consciousness, hinting at a deeper story yet to unfold. Paul understood that this was not just about healing his leg, but about uncovering the truth and understanding the events that had led to his injury. It was a journey that would test his resilience and courage, but one that he was determined to undertake.

As he drifted back into sleep, Paul felt a sense of resolve. He would face the shadows, uncover the secrets, and emerge stronger on the other side. His carefree summer days might have been interrupted, but his spirit remained unbroken, ready to take on whatever challenges lay ahead.

Paul's Journey of Resilience

Paul began the arduous process of rehabilitation, it became clear that things would never be the same. The doctor's words to his mother echoed in Paul's mind: "If he grows to a certain height, he will always walk with a limp. The fracture will never fully heal, and his leg won't grow as it should." It was a prognosis that struck at the heart of Paul's dreams. The injury would leave a permanent mark, a reminder of the fragility of the human body.

Despite the grim news, Paul was determined to regain his former agility. He worked tirelessly to strengthen his leg, pushing through the pain and frustration. Over time, his muscles grew stronger, and he regained some of his speed, but it was clear that he would never be the same as before. The pain in his ankle persisted, a constant reminder of the limitations imposed by his injury.

Paul had to adjust his expectations and find new ways to excel. His once effortless flips and tumbles were now accompanied by sharp pain, and his speed, though still impressive, was no longer unmatched. He remembered the days when no one could outrun him, but now, he found himself being outpaced by others who had once lagged behind. It was a humbling experience, one that forced Paul to confront his new reality.

His father, who had been a constant source of encouragement and support, also struggled with the changes in Paul's abilities. The bond they shared through their mutual love of sports and competition was tested as Paul grappled with his limitations. The days of effortlessly faking out opponents on the field were gone, replaced by a cautious approach to avoid further injury.

Childhood Struggles

The broken foot was more than a physical setback; it was a catalyst that challenged Paul's mental acuity and resilience. The cast came off, but the pain persisted, and he found his speed and agility permanently diminished. Every attempt at regaining his former prowess brought sharp pain in his ankle, a constant reminder of his limitations. The doctors warned that if he grew to a certain height, he would always walk with a limp due to the fracture never fully healing, impacting his leg's growth. This prognosis was a heavy blow to Paul, who had been accustomed to excelling effortlessly in physical activities.

Paul's childhood was already fraught with challenges. His mother, deeply involved in the streets, struggled to provide a stable home environment. Despite her hardships, she instilled in Paul the importance of education and doing the right thing, even if she couldn't always follow her own advice. Paul, however, was often influenced by his surroundings and his mother's lifestyle, finding himself caught between her guidance and the allure of the streets.

Academically, Paul was a bright student. He consistently earned straight A's and made the honor roll, often appearing on the presidential list. His academic prowess, however, was complicated by his family dynamics. His brother, threatened by Paul's success, would pressure their mother to hold Paul back in school, fearing Paul would surpass him. As a result, Paul was held back multiple times, stunting his academic progression and creating frustration and confusion.

Paul's high school years were marked by turmoil. Initially excelling in the eighth grade, he faced constant disruptions due to his brother's conflicts. When his brother got into fights, Paul often intervened, leading to his own expulsion from school. This cycle of instability continued as he moved from one school to another, each time dealing with new challenges and setbacks.

He was set to attend Lane Tech College Prep, one of Chicago's top academic high schools. However, due to a night out with friends, he missed the crucial acceptance meeting. This missed opportunity forced him to attend a neighborhood school, Sumner, which was notorious for its rough environment. Fights, gang activity, and a lack of academic focus characterized the school, further hindering Paul's progress.

Paul's father eventually intervened, transferring him to Lincoln Park High School. However, due to jurisdictional issues and inconsistencies in his academic record from Sumner, Paul's stay at Lincoln Park was short-lived. He then tried to attend Lane Tech once more, but jurisdictional issues forced him to leave again. Finally, Paul ended up in an alternative school, a last resort that provided a semblance of stability but also underscored the chaotic journey he had endured.

Turbulence

Paul's life was a tapestry of trials, woven with threads of resilience and hope. He spent a significant part of his education at an alternative school, a place where students often landed when traditional paths failed them. Between 1990 and 1991, Paul was there, working hard to earn double credits. The possibility of graduating early was within his grasp. However, the environment was rife with gang activity, a perilous backdrop that complicated his pursuit of an education.

Despite his efforts to keep his head down and focus on his studies, Paul found it increasingly difficult to stay clear of the gang influence that pervaded the alternative school. His family had a long history with gangs, and the pull was strong. Many of his relatives were involved, and Paul had been familiar with the lifestyle from a young age. His grandfather, a pastor with a church on Harrison and California in Chicago, provided a sanctuary for Paul, but even there, the influence of gangs loomed large.

Paul's initiation into gang life began earlier than most knew. At twelve, he was already involved, though he kept this part of his life hidden from many. The gang presence around his grandfather's church was significant, and Paul, while participating in the church choir, was also subtly absorbed into the gang culture. The duality of his existence

—choir boy by day, gang affiliate by night—was a precarious balance that Paul managed with caution.

As Paul grew older, the stakes became higher. His life at the alternative school was a microcosm of the larger gang culture. The gangs knew of his family ties and eventually, his own affiliations. The school, intended as a refuge for troubled teens, instead became another battlefield. Paul's presence there lit up the gang's radar, making it unsafe for him to remain. He had to leave, yet another disruption in his tumultuous educational journey.

Paul's decision to join the gang was influenced by a sense of belonging and the protection it offered. In his world, gang affiliation was almost a rite of passage, a means of survival. His family's entanglement in gang life made it seem inevitable. When Paul faced threats and challenges at school, joining a gang seemed like the only way to secure his safety and find camaraderie in a hostile environment.

However, Paul's connection to the gang was not merely about protection. There was also a deep sense of loyalty and identity. The gang provided a structure and a sense of purpose that was missing in other parts of his life. Paul was torn between the destructive allure of gang life and his aspirations for a better future.

Chapter 3

The Unfolding Nightmare Of Daniel Taylor

Navigating a Hostile World

December 3, 1992, was a day that forever changed the life of Daniel Taylor. At just 17 years old, Daniel was a typical teenager who enjoyed boxing and being an active member of his community. But his upbringing was anything but ordinary. Daniel's parents struggled with drug addiction, which led to his placement with the Department of Children and Family Services (DCFS). As a ward of the state, Daniel spent his formative years moving through various foster homes and group homes across Illinois.

By the age of 16, Daniel found himself in a group home called MYS, an independent living program designed to prepare adolescents for adulthood. This program aimed to equip young people with the skills needed to transition into independent living. It was here that Daniel learned essential life skills such as budgeting, paying rent, job application processes, and how to secure an apartment. The goal was to ensure that by the time he left the program, he would be ready to face the world as a self-sufficient adult.

During this pivotal time, Daniel met Paul Phillips, a friendship that would prove to be a significant part of his life. Paul and Daniel quickly became close friends, often spending time at each other's home, playing games, and engaging in the typical activities of teenage boys. Despite the challenges of his upbringing, Daniel had his own apartment through the DCFS program, which allowed him a certain degree of independence that many of his peers did not have.

Through Paul, Daniel met Paul's brother, Akia Phillips, and another friend, Lewis Gardner. The four young men formed a tight-knit group, spending their days exploring their neighborhood, having fun, and supporting each other. This camaraderie was a source of stability and joy for Daniel amidst the turbulence of his life in the foster care system.

However, the sense of normalcy that Daniel had worked so hard to build was shattered on that fateful December morning. Awakened abruptly in his group home, Daniel's life took an unexpected turn. The specifics of what transpired that day are a blur, but the impact was profound and life-altering.

One night, a particular incident tested Daniel's resilience to its core. On December 3rd, he was staying at a group home called CYS after being kicked out of the independent living program. He was abruptly awakened around 2 or 3 in the morning by police officers. They didn't wake him up by his name, but rather by calling him "Black T," a nickname that struck him as odd and unsettling.

Groggy and disoriented, Daniel responded, "Yeah, that's me. What's up?" The officers identified themselves and stated they needed to take him down for questioning. Confused and concerned, Daniel repeatedly asked why they needed to question him, but they never provided an answer. They simply instructed him to get dressed and follow them.

As Daniel walked out of the DCFS place with the officers, he questioned the staff members about why they were allowing this to happen. The staff replied that the officers wanted to take him down for questioning and had been given permission to do so. Feeling a mixture of anxiety and frustration, Daniel got into the police car, still unsure about what was happening.

The ride to the police station was a blur. Daniel's mind raced with questions and fears. What could they possibly want with him? Had something happened to someone he knew? Was he being wrongly

The Unfolding Nightmare Of Daniel Taylor

accused of something? The silence of the officers did nothing to alleviate his concerns. They seemed intent on keeping him in the dark, which only heightened his sense of unease.

Upon arriving at the police station, Daniel was led into a stark, brightly lit room. The harsh lighting made the atmosphere even more intimidating. He was seated at a table, and the questioning began. Despite his repeated inquiries, the officers remained evasive, offering no clear reason for his detention. The hours dragged on as they asked him about his whereabouts and activities, but the purpose of the interrogation remained unclear.

Chapter 4

The Relentless Sacrifices Of Lewis Gardner

Early Life and Introduction to the Streets

Lewis's story began down south, where he spent his early childhood in a relatively stable environment. However, this stability was short-lived. His mother, seeking a better life or possibly escaping something left unspoken, moved the family to Chicago. Lewis, the middle child with two sisters, found himself in a new and daunting world. It was in Chicago that he reconnected with Paul, a friend who lived just down the street.

The streets of Chicago became their playground, and unfortunately, their battleground, with their mother's constantly at work.Lewis and Paul found themselves unsupervised and exposed to the harsh realities of street life.

Lewis's early years were marred by his mother's drug addiction. The realization that his mother was using drugs and the consequent instability it brought to their home life was a harsh awakening for him. The situation came to a head when his sister's abusive boyfriend became a threat. In an attempt to protect his sister, who was pregnant at the time, Lewis confronted the boyfriend. This act of defiance led to his mother kicking him out of the house, leaving him to fend for himself on the streets.

Finding himself homeless, Lewis sought refuge wherever he could. He ended up staying with Paul, trying to make ends meet through any means possible. Despite his precarious situation, he never stopped caring for his family. He worked tirelessly, doing various odd jobs including selling drugs, and would send the money he earned back home. He made sure his sister had school supplies, his nephew had diapers, and there was milk in the house. His selflessness and sense of responsibility were unwavering, even when his own circumstances were dire.

Life on the streets was brutal. Lewis often found himself caught between juvenile detention and the penitentiary, a cycle that seemed unbreakable. He faced arrest five times, each stint behind bars a stark reminder of the narrow margins within which he was forced to live. Yet, these experiences did not break him; instead, they fueled his resolve to keep going, to keep fighting for a better future.

At just fourteen, Lewis had to drop out of school in the eighth grade. Education became a distant dream as survival took precedence. He turned to the streets, where he hustled to make a living. From selling sandwiches made in a makeshift kitchen to taking on any odd job that came his way, Lewis did whatever was necessary to get by. The streets became his classroom, teaching him hard lessons about resilience, resourcefulness, and grit.

Amidst the chaos of his life, Lewis found a small measure of comfort in poetry. Writing became an outlet for his emotions, a way to process the turmoil and express his innermost thoughts. It was through poetry that he could momentarily escape the harsh realities of his existence and dream of a different life.

Descent into Gang Life

With no one to guide or protect them, Lewis and Paul began associating with the wrong crowd. The allure of gang life, with its promise of camaraderie and financial gain, was irresistible to young boys left to fend for themselves. They observed older gang members, idolizing their apparent control over their environment and their ability to generate income. The idea of relying on themselves for money and protection was appealing, and so they joined the ranks of the gang.

Lewis's introduction to gang life was not an abrupt plunge but a gradual immersion. He started small, running errands and learning the ropes from the older members. Over time, as he and Paul gained confidence, they began to undertake more significant tasks. This involvement, however, came with its own set of dangers and consequences.

Lewis quickly learned that life in a gang was fraught with peril. The constant threat of violence, run-ins with the law, and the harsh reality of street survival became his daily existence. Despite this, he remained steadfast in his resolve to protect and provide for his family. His mother's absence due to work left a void that he felt compelled to fill, especially for his younger sister.

Lewis's life was a delicate balance of navigating the treacherous gang landscape while trying to maintain some semblance of normalcy for his family. He used the money he earned from gang activities to ensure that his sister had school supplies and his nephew had essentials like diapers and milk. This sense of responsibility kept him grounded, even as he became more deeply entangled in the gang's operations.

Throughout his teenage years, Lewis faced numerous run-ins with the law. Arrests, juvenile detention, and eventually time in the penitentiary became part of his life. Each arrest was a stark reminder of the narrow margins within which he lived. However, these experiences also taught him resilience and resourcefulness. He learned to navigate a world that was often hostile, using every setback as a lesson in survival.

Despite the constant challenges, Lewis never lost sight of his responsibilities. He continued to provide for his family, even from behind bars. His resilience was not just physical but emotional and mental. He developed a tough exterior to cope with the violence and unpredictability of gang life, yet he maintained a deep sense of care and duty towards his family.

Chapter 5

The Frame-Up

Organization of False Confessions

By November 1992, Agitate Ave had become a notorious hub for the Vice Lord Gang, a place where drug dealers and addicts mingled in a haze of uncertainty and fear. From the outside, it was impossible to distinguish who was who, but the gang ruled with an iron fist, particularly on the north side. Here, teenage boys seeking protection found themselves molded into hardened members of the Vice Lords.

Among the ranks were Dennis Mixon, known as Goldie, C-Deon, Black T, and Rock. Goldie, a Traveling Vice Lord from the west side of Chicago, had risen to the rank of chief. He controlled the cocaine trade on the north side, particularly in Sunnyside and Agitate Streets. It was a cold November 16th when the Vice Lords convened a crucial meeting at Clarendon Park, scheduled from 7:00 to 7:30 p.m., to address pressing issues involving drug money.

As the members gathered, the tension was palpable. Everyone was present, including Black T, who had recently been released from jail. The main topic of discussion was a debt owed by Jeffrey Lassiter.

"The main problem is that Jeffrey Lassiter owes us money," Goldie declared, his voice steady but filled with underlying menace.

"If we don't get the money, I'll take care of it!" C-Deon exclaimed, dramatically pulling a pistol from his belt.

Rock, as the rank chief of the north side Traveling Vice Lords, directed the meeting with an authoritative air. Goldie suspected that C-Deon would either scare Jeffrey into paying up or shoot him in the leg to make a point. With the meeting concluded, it was time to confront Jeffrey. Rock assigned four Vice Lords to act as lookouts. Their task was simple: if the police approached, they were to yell "Five-O" or "Dianna."

The group moved with purpose from Clarendon Park down Agitate Ave toward Jeffrey's building. Upon arrival, the lookouts dispersed while Rock, C-Deon, Black T, and Goldie made their way to the front entrance. They rang the doorbell to 910 W. Agitate, and someone buzzed them in. The four men ascended to the second floor, their footsteps echoing ominously in the stairwell. Once they stood in front of Jeffrey's door, Rock knocked loudly: *Bang-Bang-Bang*. There was no response. Impatient and angry, they kicked the door down with a resounding *Boom-Boom-Boom*.

Inside, Jeffrey was in the front room, and Sharon was in the bathroom. Rock wasted no time.

"Goldie and Black T, y'all go to the bathroom and get her out!" Rock commanded.

Black T and Goldie approached the bathroom door, their voices stern. "Come out now!" they demanded.

"I'm using the restroom," Sharon replied, her voice shaking.

"COME OUT NOW!" they repeated, louder this time.

Slowly, Sharon opened the door. Black T and Goldie grabbed her by the arms and dragged her to the bedroom, forcing her to sit on the couch. Meanwhile, Rock and C-Deon confronted Jeffrey.

"Where's our money?" Rock demanded.

"I don't have it," Jeffrey stammered, his voice trembling.

Fury erupted in Rock as he began hitting Jeffrey, his fists flying. C-Deon joined in, yelling about the money. When their efforts yielded no information, C-Deon turned his rage toward Sharon, striking her as Black T and Goldie held her down.

"I don't know anything about any money!" Sharon cried, her voice breaking with fear and pain.

The Frame-Up

Desperation flashed in C-Deon's eyes as he pulled out his gun and pointed it at Jeffrey. Without hesitation, he fired twice. Sharon screamed, pleading for her life.

"Please don't shoot me!" she begged, tears streaming down her face.

C-Deon turned the gun towards her. "You know what happened here, so you have to go too," he said coldly. A few trigger clicks later, Sharon lay lifeless beside Jeffrey, blood pooling around their bodies, a grim testament to the Vice Lords' ruthless control over Agitate Ave.

Rock, his face impassive, walked over to Jeffrey and began to search his pockets. His fingers rifled through the fabric until they found a crumpled wad of cash. He pulled out $200, shaking his head at the paltry sum. "This ain't enough," he muttered, pocketing the money anyway.

"Let's get outta here," Rock ordered, and the men began to make their way out of the apartment. They moved quickly, knowing they had to vanish before anyone got suspicious. They exited the building, the cold November air hitting their faces as they stepped onto the street.

Goldie split off from the group, heading west on Agitate towards Sheridan, intending to lay low at his mother's place on Lake Street. Rock, C-Deon, and Black T walked east, their footsteps echoing in the silent night. The gravity of their actions lingered in the air like a dark cloud.

Minutes later, the wail of sirens broke the stillness as the coroners arrived at the scene. Inside the apartment, they found Jeffrey's body, cold and lifeless. But to their surprise, Sharon was still alive, though barely. She lay in a pool of her own blood, clinging to life with every shallow breath.

Medical examiners rushed to her side, immediately beginning to treat her injuries. Sharon had suffered multiple gunshot wounds, each more horrific than the last. The most grievous wound was to her left cheek, involving the mastoid bone. Evidence of close-range firing was clear around the entry wound. A deformed lead bullet was recovered from within her left petrous temporal bone, having coursed from left to right, anterior to posterior, in a straight path that caused severe contusions to her brain.

Another bullet had entered at the left corner of her mouth,

wreaking havoc as it tore through her tongue, teeth, and left orbit. This wound was even more brutal; a fully copper-jacketed, medium-caliber lead bullet was found lodged in the superior aspect of her left orbit. Sharon's face was a canvas of violence, with a sutured laceration on the left side of her forehead and a superficial abrasion on her right knee adding to the grim portrait.

Despite the efforts to save her, the severity of her injuries was insurmountable. Sharon was pronounced dead shortly after arriving at the hospital. She was 29 years old, another tragic victim of the merciless streets ruled by the Vice Lords. Her death, marked by its brutality, would linger in the minds of those who knew her and stand as a somber reminder of the cost of crossing the gang that dominated Agitate Ave.

In the aftermath, as news of the incident spread, fear tightened its grip on the community. Agitate Ave remained a battleground, its residents caught in the crossfire of the ruthless and relentless pursuit of power and money by the Vice Lords. And for those who lived in the shadow of the gang, the line between life and death seemed thinner than ever.

Chapter 6

The Round Up

It was November 16, 1992, Paul had just returned from Texas the night before and was at his mom's house. Excited to catch up with his friends, he first walked to Lewis's house around 5:30 pm, only to be told by Lewis's mom that he was not there. He then walked east towards the park district to see if his friends were playing basketball, but he didn't find anyone there. As Paul was leaving Clarendon Park, he ran into his two friends, Carick and Mohammad, who had just gotten into a fight with some guys who had jumped them. As they were talking, Black T showed up, and Paul began telling him what had happened to Mohammad. They all started walking west towards the alley and ended up encountering the guys who had jumped Mohammad. They approached them to question their actions but couldn't address the situation as they wanted because the guys had their moms and aunts around them, who kept shouting for them to leave. Paul and his friends hung around until the women shouted that they had called the police. The guys started running down the alley, and moments later, the police arrived. Everyone made a run for it, but the police grabbed Daniel (Black T), Paul, Carick, and Mohammad turned right down the alley towards their respective homes. It was after 6 pm when Paul made it back home. His mom's friend, Fluff, and her son were hanging out in the living room. Paul went to his room to watch television, enjoying "The Fresh Prince of Bel-Air," followed by Monday night football and wrestling.

The doorbell rang, and it was his friend Mark. They walked around to the back porch to talk and were shooting the ball into the Nerf basketball rim. Eventually, the ball fell downstairs, and Mark went to retrieve it. As Mark was grabbing the ball, Paul saw a bunch of lights coming from the alley area. All of a sudden, Paul heard his moms friend Fluff calling his name to come inside. When he walked into the dining room, the police were there waiting for him.

"Freeze!" the officer yelled.

Everyone was escorted out while the police searched the place. Paul could see an officer walking into his bedroom, where they found some drugs. When they placed the drugs on the table, Paul's mother was upset and in disbelief. As the police proceeded with their process, there was a knock at the door. The officer instructed everyone to be quiet. When he opened the door, it was Deon and his friend. The officer brought them inside and shortly after told my mom to get dressed. The officer walked over to Paul.

"Where's the gun?" he asked.

Fluff's three-year-old son replied, "I know where a gun is."

The officers followed him into the bedroom where the young boy pointed at the alleged weapon, which turned out to be a toy flashlight mistaken for a gun. The officer then took Paul's mom downstairs, put her in the car, and took her to the police station while everyone else was left inside the apartment. This wasn't the first time her place had been raided for drugs, so she was no stranger to the game. Paul walked over to the window to watch what was going on and saw Black T walking down the street, so he assumed the other officers had released him. Usually, Black T had to walk past his apartment to get home, but Black T never appeared again. Later, Paul's mom called him from the police station to tell him about her bond and shared that Black T had told the officers where the drugs were in the apartment, and that he was no longer allowed to visit and spend the night. When Black T came around later that night, Paul told him what his mom said, but Black T denied telling

The Round Up

the police anything. Paul wasn't sure if it was true or not. Paul and Black T ended up going to the store and then back to the apartment. An hour later, Akia and Lewis bailed his mom out of jail.

On a crisp November 29th, the murder investigation was at a standstill. The officers had no suspects, no leads, and no clear path forward. But desperation drives men to questionable lengths, and this case was no different. Despite having no suspects, officers on their day off took the initiative to order a set of photographs, ostensibly to aid in their investigation. By December 2nd, they had these pictures in hand—a stack of images that would soon be manipulated to fit their narrative. The phone rang early in the morning, and Paul's mother answered. She called Paul on the phone because a guy named Ed was looking for work. Paul knew Ed because they were in the same gang. Paul, Akia, and Lewis headed out to meet with him. Lewis, Akia (Baby T), and Paul had just left to sell drugs that morning. As they walked down the alley towards the street, the police suddenly surrounded them. They didn't even have a chance to run. The officers put them against the wall to search them, and everyone started throwing their drugs on the ground. Paul kept walking as this was happening, but eventually, they grabbed him too.

"Where were you headed?" the officer asked.

"I was headed to the store to grab my mom some eggs and bread," Paul replied.

The officer searched his pockets and only found 20 dollars. Eventually, they sat him down with Lewis and Akia, searched the perimeter, and found 150 dime bags discarded on the ground. They were shoved into the back of a police car and taken to Addison and Halsted, where they were charged with drugs. At the station, they pinned 75 bags on Lewis and 75 bags on Akia and released Paul, giving him a ticket for disorderly conduct. When Paul got back to the apartment, his brother Akia called. Akia always lied about his age because he looked younger, hence his nickname Baby T. He told the officers he was 12 years old, which allowed him to call home, but his mom refused to come get him, so Akia had to stay the night.

That evening, police returned for Paul, taking him back to the station without handcuffs. During the ride, an officer asked when Paul had last shot a gun, to which Paul replied he didn't shoot guns. At the station, Paul noticed his brother's jacket before being placed in an interrogation room, where he eventually fell asleep awaiting further questioning.

Chapter 7

Say This, Sign Here

Lewis was separated from the others, putting him in a room while they called his mom, who was at work at the time. When she arrived, worry etched deep into her face, they kept asking him the same thing over and over. But Lewis kept telling them, "I don't know." One youth officer, he wasn't even sure what she was, kept pressing. His mom walked in, and they told her, "You need to tell him to say something." But he didn't know anything about the murder.

They told Lewis he was supposed to go home, but then another officer said the detectives wanted to talk to him. They took them all down to Belmont and Western. When we got there, Lewis told his mom, "We didn't even walk in the door all the way." His mom had to go back to work, so they took him upstairs in an elevator to an interview room. Lewis kept telling them, "I don't know anything about the murder. I thought I was here for drugs." They left him there for a while, and he just sat in that room with no windows until he fell asleep on the floor.

A detective came in, blowing smoke from his Marlboro cigarettes in Lewis' face. "Tell me something," he said.

"I want to go home. I want to see my mom," Lewis replied.

"You can't see anyone until you tell me something," he replied.

Lewis then repeated, "I don't know anything." More people came in, one of them claiming to be Lewis' lawyer. Since his mom wasn't there, Lewis assumed his mom had gotten him a lawyer, but he was actually a detective.

"I'm your attorney. You have to tell me something," the man said.

Lewis maintained his same response, "I don't know anything about a murder."

Hours passed by. Lewis was exhausted and ready to go home. They came back in with a bunch of pictures and papers.

"I want you to read the papers," the man said.

"I can't read that good," Lewis replied.

"You're lying to me," he said

"I'm not lying to you!" Lewis exclaimed. "I can't read. I went to school up until 8th grade but I was in the streets a lot and was barely home."

The man came in with the papers. "I'm going to read these off to you, then I want you to put them into your own words."

"I don't know what it is," Lewis continued.

"If you say this and put your initials, we will let you go home," he replied.

"Okay."

They left the room and came back in with this woman who had a stenographic machine to capture the testimony of the proceedings as the court reporter. The room was crowded now—Assistant State's Attorney Martin Fogarty, Detective Villardita, the court reporter, youth officer Heryman, and Lewis Gardner.

Fogarty started, "What do you know about the murder of Jeffrey Lassiter and Sharon Haugabook, which occurred on November 16, 1992, at approximately 8:43 pm at 910 West Agatite in Chicago?"

"I don't know nothing about a murder. I thought I was in here for drugs," I replied.

"Lewis, I talked to you earlier and explained that I am an Assistant State's Attorney, a lawyer and prosecutor, and not your lawyer, is that correct?" Fogarty asked.

"Yes, sir."

"And before we spoke, I advised you of your constitutional rights, is that correct?"

"Yes, sir."

"I am going to read your rights again. Do you understand that you have the right to remain silent?"

"Yes, sir."

"Do you understand you have the right to talk to a lawyer and have him present with you while you are being questioned?"

"Yes, sir."

"Do you understand if you cannot afford to hire a lawyer, and you want one, a lawyer will be appointed by the court to represent you before any questioning?"

"Yes, sir."

"Do you understand that you will be treated and charged as an adult in this case?"

"Yes, sir."

"Understanding these rights, do you wish to talk to us now?"

"Yeah."

"Excuse me?"

"Yes, sir."

"Lewis, please state your full name and spell your last name?"

"Lewis Gardner, G-A-R-D-N-E-R."

"How old are you, Lewis?"

"Fifteen."

"What is your birthday?"

"September 8, 1977."

"What is your present address?"

"4408 North Hazel."

"Who do you live with?"

"My mother."

"Anyone else?"

"My two sisters, and my stepfather."

"Where do you go to school?"

"Senn."

"What year are you at Senn?"

"First."

"Freshman?"

"Yeah."

"Lewis, are you a member of a gang?"

"Yes, sir."

"What gang is that?"

"Vice Lords."

"How long have you been a member of the Vice Lords?"

"For about two years."

"Do you have a rank in the Vice Lords?"

"No, sir."

"Lewis, I want to draw your attention to the date of November 16, 1992, at about 7:00 pm. Do you remember that day?"

"Yes, sir."

"Did you have occasion that day to be at Clarendon Park in Chicago?"

"Yes, sir."

"Where is Clarendon Park?"

"It's Clarendon and Sunnyside."

"What were you doing in Clarendon Park that night?"

"We were having a gang meeting."

"Can you tell me who was present at the gang meeting?"

"It was C-Deon, Paul Phillips, Deon Phillips, Rock, Ed, Slick, T Mack, Black T, Cuzzo, and that's all I can remember."

"Do you recall—"

"And me."

"You were there?"

"Yeah."

"Do you recall if someone named Pookie was there?"

"Yeah."

"Was Pookie there?"

"Yes, sir."

"Do you recall if someone named Goldie was there?"

"Yeah."

"Was Goldie there?"

"Yes, sir."

"I have in my hand what's been marked Exhibit No. 1. Can you identify that exhibit, what that is?"

"This is Maryville Children's Home right here."

"Is Exhibit No. 1 a map?"

"Yes, sir."

"Okay, and Maryville is the children's home you just pointed to. It would be located on that map somewhere, is that correct?"

"Yes, sir."

"Can you put a No. 1 where you had your meeting at Clarendon Park, where you had your gang meeting?"

"Right behind the fieldhouse."

"I also have in my hand several photographs, and I'm going to mark them as exhibits. I'm going to show them to you and ask you if you recognize the people in those photographs and if you do, tell me and identify them if you would. I have in my hand Exhibit No. 2."

"That's C-Deon."

"Do you know C-Deon's full name?"

"No, sir."

"You only know him as C-Deon?"

"Yeah."

"How do you know him?"

"I see him walking up and down the street and keep on going."

"Is he in your gang?"

"He's in a different gang, but he's a Vice Lord also."

"Does he have a rank in the Vice Lords?"

"Yes, sir."

"What's his rank?"

"Chief."

"How do you know that?"

"Because he tells a lot of the Vice Lords what to do."

"Does he tell you what to do?"

"Uh-huh."

"Do you see the IR number in the photo, Exhibit No. 2?"

"Yes, sir."

"What is that number?"

"908357."

"That last number is one, not a seven?"

"Yes, sir."

"I have in my hand another photo. This is Exhibit No. 3. Do you recognize who is in this photo?"

"Yes, sir."

"Who is this?"

"That's Paul Phillips."

"How do you recognize Paul Phillips? How do you know him?"

"We grew up together."

"Was he at the gang meeting?"

"Yes, sir."

"I have in my hand Exhibit No. 4. Do you recognize the person in this exhibit?"

"Yes, sir."

"Who is that?"

"That's Deon Phillips."

"Do you know Deon Phillips?"

"Yes, sir."

"How do you know Deon Phillips?"

"We grew up together."

"Is he related to Paul Phillips?"

"They're brothers."

"Does Deon Phillips have a nickname?"

"Baby T."

"I have in my hand Exhibit No. 5. Do you recognize who is in that photo?"

"Yes, sir."

"Who is that?"

"Daniel Taylor."

"How do you know Daniel Taylor?"

"He used to live with Paul Phillips."

"Does Daniel Taylor have a nickname?"

"Yes, sir."

"What's his nickname?"

"Black T."

"I have in my hand what's marked Exhibit No. 6. Do you recognize the person in this photograph?"

"Yes, sir."

"Who is that?"

"Goldie."

"Do you know what Goldie's full name is?"

"No, sir."

"Do you see the number next to that, the IR number in this photograph?"

"Yes, sir."

"Can you read that number?"

"678832."

"Was Goldie at that meeting?"

"Yes, sir."

"I have in my hand what's marked Exhibit No. 7. Do you recognize the person in this photo?"

"Yes, sir."

"Who is that person?"

"Rock."

"Do you know Rock by any other name?"

"No, sir."

"How do you know Rock?"

"He's a chief of the Travelers."

"What does that mean?"

"He's the chief of the Vice Lords, Traveler Vice Lords."

"He's one of the leaders of the Vice Lords?"

"Yes, sir."

"Do you see an IR number on this, attached to this person Rock?"

"Yes, sir."

"What is Rock's IR number?"

"9102815."

"Okay. Is that the IR number or the CB number?"

"824772."

"The first number that you read, 9102815, what number was that?"

"CB."

"Was Rock at that meeting on November 16th?"

The Hazel Boyz

"Yes, sir."

"I have in my hand Exhibit No. 8. Do you recognize the person in this photo?"

"Yes, sir."

"Who is this person?"

"Cuzzo."

"And how long have you known Cuzzo?"

"Since we moved around here."

"How long is that?"

"That's since February."

"And how is it that you know Cuzzo?"

"We talk on the street."

"Is Cuzzo also a Vice Lord?"

"Yes, sir."

"Was Cuzzo at that meeting?"

"Yes, sir."

"Can you read Cuzzo's ID number as it appears on Exhibit No. 8?"

"909224."

"On Exhibit No. 1, you indicated where your gang meeting took place, and that was by the fieldhouse at Clarendon Park, is that correct?"

"Behind."

"Behind the fieldhouse?"

"Yes, sir."

"How were you congregated at the fieldhouse?"

"We were all standing in a circle right there." Lewis mentioned as he drew a circle to the east of the fieldhouse, indicating where they were standing.

"And was anyone talking at the meeting?" Fogarty continued.

"Yes, sir."

"Who was talking?"

"C-Deon and Rock."

"Where were C-Deon and Rock?"

"They were in the middle of the circle."

"Were they both in the circle at the same time?"

"C-Deon was in there first."

"What did he say when he was in the middle, if anything?"

"He said some people owe him some money, and he wanted—he said they kept beating him up, and he never did get the money."

"You said they kept beating him up. Who was beating who up?"

"C-Deon and Rock were beating the people that owed them some money."

"Who were the people that owed C-Deon and Rock money?"

"I don't remember their names."

"Okay. Do you know where these people lived?"

"They lived on Agatite."

"Do you know where on Agatite?"

"Uh-huh."

"What else did C-Deon say?"

"He said he wanted something done to them."

"Did C-Deon say how much money this person owed him?"

"He said about three or four hundred dollars."

"Did C-Deon say what would happen if this person didn't pay him the money?"

"He said he was going to shoot him."

"What else did C-Deon do?"

"That's it."

"Did C-Deon show anything?"

"Yes, he showed a gun. After the meeting, we went to the fieldhouse, and he showed a gun. I didn't get a good look at it. I just saw the black. He had it beside his beltline. He flashed it out for a minute and then put it back in."

Lewis kept repeating, "I don't know anything about the murder," hoping the words would set him free.

In the early hours of December 4, 1992, Paul was abruptly awakened in his room by a police officer. Disoriented and groggy, he was immediately faced with a barrage of questions. The officer, pressing for answers, bluntly asked, "Who did the murder?" Paul, confused and caught off guard, denied knowing anything about the incident. The officer left the room, leaving Paul increasingly frustrated and anxious as he glanced at the clock, which read just past 1 AM.

Moments later, the door swung open again, and Assistant State's Attorney Martin Fogarty entered the room, accompanied by Detective

Johnson and court reporter Annette Faklis. The time was 1:33 AM, and the weight of the situation began to settle on Paul. Fogarty started the interrogation, confirming Paul's age and living situation.

"Paul, how old are you?" Fogarty asked.

"Seventeen," Paul responded.

"Who do you live with?"

"My mom, Andrea Phillips."

The questions soon turned towards Paul's affiliations, revealing a more complex situation.

"Paul, are you a member of a gang?"

"Yes, Vice Lords," Paul admitted.

"How long have you been a member?"

"About a month."

The interrogation continued, focusing on the events of November 16, 1992, at Clarendon Park, seeking details about the night's meeting.

Chapter 8

Conspired Confessions

In the stark atmosphere of a dimly lit interrogation room, Paul found himself handcuffed and surrounded by shadows and uncertainty. Earlier that night, the officers had assembled a lineup, placing Paul, Deon, Daniel, and Rodney—known as Rock—alongside other unfamiliar faces. On the other side of the glass was the acclaimed witness named Faye, a respected community leader known for organizing block parties and events that brought the neighborhood together. She was more than just a witness; she was someone who had watched most of the young men in question grow up. When the officers presented her with the lineup, they expected her to identify the young men they had already decided were guilty. But Faye's conscience and deep knowledge of her community wouldn't allow her to be coerced into a false identification. She carefully examined the faces in the lineup, her mind replaying the events of that fateful day. The people she had seen were not the ones in the lineup before her. She told the officers as much, stating firmly that the individuals they had in custody were not the ones she saw. She pointed out the discrepancies in the descriptions, noting that the height and size of the men she saw did not match the young men in custody. Her voice, filled with certainty, should have been the final word, but it wasn't. The officers, now in too deep with their fabricated evidence, couldn't afford to let Faye's testimony dismantle their case. Despite her insistence, the officers pressed on with their story. They couldn't allow Faye's truth to undo their work. Her statement was quietly buried, and the case proceeded as if she had never spoken. After a tense silence, an officer entered, announcing that a witness had identified them all. This revelation plunged Paul deeper into confusion and fear, particularly as the officers separated them into different rooms.

Throughout the night, officers would enter Paul's room, using physical intimidation and shining flashlights in his face, disrupting his uneasy sleep. Each time, the interaction left Paul more anxious and disoriented. In a desperate search for clarity, he prayed, hoping for some understanding of the situation that had engulfed him. During one such intrusive visit, Paul caught sight of another individual, Daniel, in a neighboring room. The officer's harsh words shattered the silence, accusing Paul of being implicated in a murder—a crime he knew nothing about. As the weight of the accusation pressed down on him, Paul's mind raced, struggling to comprehend the gravity of the situation. The officers continued to assert that "everyone" was implicating him, using this collective accusation to break his resolve. The officers also used other tactics by showing Paul other statements signed by others. The officers stated that everyone said Paul did the crime and Paul would be going to jail for the rest of his life or get the death penalty if Paul doesn't cooperate.

Paul sat with his head down, his thoughts a chaotic jumble as the detectives' voices droned on around him. They stepped out of the room, leaving him in the cold, sterile silence, only to return with the same menacing tone. Flashlights glared in his eyes, blinding him momentarily as they repeated, "You will cooperate."

The relentless pressure weighed heavily on Paul. He felt trapped, confused, and scared. The detectives employed a ruthless barrage of threats and promises, each one more terrifying than the last. "You'll never see your mother again," they warned. "You'll never see the light of day again. Do you know how much time people get for this? They get life. Some even get the death penalty."

Paul's heart pounded in his chest as their words sank in. They pushed him back into his chair, ordering him to keep his head down.

Conspired Confessions

Desperation clawed at him. The idea of going home was a distant dream he clung to amidst the rising tide of fear. The mention of severe consequences—life imprisonment or even the death penalty—terrified Paul, a mere 17-year-old facing an incomprehensible reality. Paul's fear and confusion made him vulnerable, caught in a psychological battle between the officers' intimidating tactics and his own disbelieving mind. He felt trapped, with the officers' threats echoing ominously in the room, leaving him to wonder if he would ever find a way out of this nightmare. They brought him back into the room, the same harsh lights and unyielding stares meeting him. "If you cooperate, you can go home," they said. Paul, a young man caught in a whirlwind of accusations and intimidation, wanted to believe them. The thought of freedom, of seeing his family again, was too tempting to resist.

When they handed him the statement, he hesitated. The papers felt heavy in his hands, each page a potential trap. "Sign here," they instructed. "Put your initials there." With trembling hands, Paul did as he was told, each stroke of the pen feeling like a surrender. He signed where they pointed, initials marking the spots they indicated. He didn't fully understand the gravity of what he was doing. He was overwhelmed, trying to navigate a situation far beyond his comprehension. The detectives offered no real clarity, only a stark choice between cooperation and an eternity behind bars. Once he was done, they collected the papers, their expressions unreadable. Paul felt a flicker of hope. He had done what they asked. Maybe now he could go home. But deep down, a gnawing doubt lingered. He had signed away something important, something he might never get back. In that stark, unforgiving room, Paul realized too late that his hope for freedom had been a cruel mirage. The reality of his situation began to sink in, the weight of his decisions pressing down on him like a vise. He had cooperated, but at what cost?

In the next room, Paul's brother Akia faced the same grueling interrogation with Assistant State's Attorney Martin Fogarty and Detective Terry O'Connor, while the court reporter documented every word.

"What did you do after Rock said to get off the strip?" they asked.

"I went home, called a cab, and went over to my girlfriend's house," Akia replied.

"Drawing your attention to the next day, did you see anyone involved in the gang meeting?"

"Rock, C-Deon, and Popeye," Akia answered.

"When you say Deon, you mean C-Deon?"

"Yes, sir."

"Where did you see them?"

"At Agatite and Hazel."

"Would you mark where you saw them, please? What happened when you were with that group?" the officer pressed.

"Rock and Deon were laughing," Akia said.

"What were they laughing about?"

"They shot somebody. Popeye and I were just standing there, not finding it funny."

"You and Popeye were not laughing, correct?"

"Yes, sir."

"Who were Rock and C-Deon talking about?"

"I don't know. They never told us the name."

"Were they talking about the event from the day before?"

"Yes, sir."

"What did C-Deon say while he was laughing?"

"He didn't say anything. He was just laughing. We kept asking what was so funny."

"And what did he eventually say?"

"That he shot somebody."

"Did he tell you anything about it?"

"No, sir. They wouldn't tell me anything because they think I'm a traitor."

The officers pushed further, suggesting that cooperation and signing a statement were his only paths to freedom. Once they had shaped the scenario, the officer proceeded to ask the final questions to wrap up the interrogation.

"Akia, has anyone promised you anything in exchange for this statement?"

"Yeah," he replied.

"What has been promised to you?"

"The police officer promised me that if I told him what happened, they would get my drug case thrown out," he stated.

The court reporter documented this into the statement, and there was no erasing these words.

"Akia, I asked you this question before, and you told me that no one promised you anything, correct?"

"I didn't think you were talking about that," Akia replied.

"Let me ask you this. Are you making this statement now because of a promise someone made to you before?"

"No, sir," Akia stated.

"Why are you making this statement now?"

"Because you're asking."

"And I didn't threaten you, did I?"

"No, sir."

"You're giving this statement freely and voluntarily, is that correct?"

"Yes, sir."

"Are you giving this statement because someone has promised you anything?"

"No, sir. They didn't find any drugs on me."

"We're not here for the drug case?"

"That's right."

"In fact, you were arrested on another case?"

"That's right."

"And that's how you came in contact with the police on this case, right?"

"Yes, sir."

"You are in custody on another case?"

"Yes, sir, I'm going back there?"

"And the police brought you in for this case?"

"Yes, sir."

"The court reporter will now type up your statement. We will read over the entire statement together, and you can make any additions or corrections you wish. Do you understand that?"

"Yes, sir."

As they reviewed Akia's statement, the inconsistencies became apparent. Akia's mention of being promised something in exchange for his statement had to be cleaned up. His responses, initially about the drug case, were twisted into the murder investigation.

To keep the story consistent, the officers hand wrote the rest of the statements, meticulously shaping the narrative they wanted. After advising Deon Patrick that Joe Mogarts was an Assistant State's Attorney and prosecutor—not his lawyer or public defender—and after advising him of his constitutional rights, Deon stated he understood each one. He then agreed to give a statement, summarized and not word for word.

Deon, a 20-year-old who could read and write English, had attended Lincoln Park High School and earned his GED. He admitted to being a member of the Conservative Vice Lords street gang for 11 years. On November 16, 1992, while on electronic monitoring with a 10:30 pm curfew, he received a call from someone known as Goldie, summoning him to a meeting of the Traveling Vice Lords street gang.

At the meeting in Clarendon Park, Goldie explained that a man who owed him money for drugs was refusing to pay, and they needed to "take care of business." This meant that if the man didn't have the money, they would have to beat him up and break his ribs. Present at the meeting were Black T, Baby T, Popeye (whose real name was Lewis), Slick, Rock (Rodney Matthews), and Carick—all members of the Traveling Vice Lords.

The group decided who would act as lookouts and who would enter the apartment. Slick, Lewis, and Baby T were designated lookouts, while Deon, Rock, Goldie, and Black T were to enter the apartment. Goldie gave Deon a silver revolver as they approached the apartment. When they arrived, Goldie knocked, and the man who owed the money let them in. Inside the apartment were a man and a girl. The girl ran out of the room as an argument about the money ensued between Goldie and the man.

Goldie then asked Deon to shoot the man. Following the command, Deon pulled the gun and shot the man in the head. The girl, who had been running, was caught by Black T and brought back into the room. Amidst Goldie's screams of "Shoot the bitch, shoot the bitch," Goldie took the gun and shot the girl himself. After both were shot, Goldie took the money from the man's pocket, and they all fled the apartment.

Conspired Confessions

Deon stated that from the apartment, he went to Andrea Phillip's house, where he encountered the police raiding the place. He was taken to the 23rd District station and then released, after which he went home to 1637 S. Springfield. During the statement, the Assistant State's Attorney showed Deon several exhibits: a photo of himself (Exhibit #2), a photo of Paul Phillips (Exhibit #3), a photo of Baby T (Exhibit #4), a photo of Black T (Exhibit #5), a photo of Goldie (Exhibit #6), a photo of Rock (Exhibit #7), and a photo of someone known as Cuzzo (Exhibit #8), who Deon confirmed was not involved in the incidents on November 16, 1992.

Deon asserted that he was treated well by both the Assistant State's Attorney and the police, claiming no promises were made to him in exchange for his statement, nor was he threatened. He stated he was allowed to eat, drink, smoke, and use the bathroom, and that he was free from the effects of drugs and alcohol.

However, beneath the surface of this supposedly voluntary confession lay a web of coercion and manipulation. The officers had systematically constructed a false confession, using Deon's fear and confusion to their advantage. As Deon signed the statement, believing it was his only path to freedom, he unknowingly sealed his fate, entrapped by the very system meant to uphold justice.

Meanwhile, another individual, Daniel Taylor, was also taken into custody from a group home known as MYS. He, too, was roused abruptly by officers in the middle of the night, around 2 or 3 AM, and brought into the ongoing investigation.

The questioning was intense, designed to extract confessions or crucial information about the murder. The late-night atmosphere added to the pressure, with the young men feeling the strain of the unexpected interrogation, unsure of what was coming next.

"Black T!" they all exclaimed at him at the same time causing him confusion at such an hour.

"Yeah, that's me," Daniel replied, still trying to gain consciousness of what was going on.

"We want to take you down for questioning," the officers stated.

"Take me down for questioning for what?" Daniel asked, but no one answered him.

"Get dressed," the officer demanded.

As he walked out of the DCFS place, he asked the staff if they knew what was going on?

"Why are y'all letting these people take me?" Daniel asked the staff person.

"They say they want to take you down for questioning," the staff person replied. "We gave them permission to come in and take you."

While Daniel waited in the back of the police car, he asked the officers again why he was being taken in for questioning. The officer let him know he would find out once they arrived at the police station. Daniel began getting frustrated.

"I don't want to go to no police station," Daniel stated. "Why are y'all taking me there?"

One of the officers grew angry with Daniel's questioning and reached into the backseat and hit him in his chest.

"Shut up!" he yelled. "You'll find out when you get there."

Once they arrived at the police station, they took Daniel to the interrogation room and handcuffed him to the wall and walked out. Shortly after, two men enter the room.

"What do you know about the murder that happened on Agatite?" the detective asked.

"I don't know of any murder that happened on Agatite," Daniel replied.

The officers were beginning to grow impatient and proceeded to ask more questions, but Daniel repeatedly mentioned his lack of knowledge of the incident.

"I know you know something," the detective said.

"I don't know nothing about no murder," Daniel stated again. "Who got killed on Agatite?"

The officer with the mustache got really aggressive with Daniel and put him in another room. Throughout the night of questioning, he saw they had Paul Phillips, Rodney Matthews, and Deon Patrick. It was at that moment I realized I wasn't alone and they had all my friends. They took me to Paul's room where I was able to ask him what was going on, but he had just as much information as I did.

"Man bro they keep talking about some murder," Paul replied.

Conspired Confessions

"Man I don't know nothing either," Daniel replied. "I'm not no killer."

The officer with the mustache came to grab Daniel out of Paul's room and took him back to the interrogation room. This time there was a court reporter present where everyone identified themselves including Assistant State's Attorney Joseph Magats, and Detective Killacky. They began the same line of questioning where Daniel answered more questions and identified other gang members. Daniel responses were one thing, but on paper something else was written to align the stories.

"What happened to the money that Rock took?" the officer asked.

"I don't know," Daniel replied.

"Where did Rock put it after he took it off of the dead guy?"

"Put it in his pocket."

"What happened after that?"

"Then they searched the girl's pocket, C Deon and Rock, they searched her back and front pockets and nothing was there."

"What did Goldie do at that time?"

"At that time, Goldie walked towards the door."

"Did goldie search the girl at all?"

"He was fiddling around?

"Around her waist."

"Where around her waist?"

"Around where, this part, the buckle part at?"

"The buckle on her pants?"

"Uh-huh" officer's implied Daniel stated.

"Did he do anything with the buckle of her pants?"

"I don't recall."

"What happened then?"

"We then exited the room that we killed the people at."

"Who exited the room?"

"Daniel Taylor, C-Deon, Rock and Goldie."

"Daniel Taylor is you, is that correct?"

"Yes."

It felt strange for Daniel to see his own name written in the third person on paper, but this was how the officers had persuaded him to frame his statements. Reluctantly, he went along with it, unsure of what else he could do in the face of their relentless pressure.

"What happened when you exited the room?"

"We stood aside from the front door, the entrance door."

"Are you talking about the front door of the apartment or the front of the building?"

"Front door to the apartment."

"What happened then?"

"That is where I was told to hide the gun."

"Who told you to hide the gun?"

"C-Deon."

"What happened then?"

"I then took the gun from C-Deon, put it in the back of my pants."

"Did you put it in anything or was it loose in your pants?"

"It was loose in my pants."

"What happened then?"

"They then said we're going to leave, and I walked out the unit first and went to the alley."

"Okay."

"I walked down, and I was going to hide it in this spot, and I then remembered my clothes came up stolen. I then walked back out from the dark spot that I was going to hide."

"Why don't we backtrack that first spot you went to hide the gun. Have you ever used that spot before?"

"Yes."

"What did you use that spot before for?"

"Clothes."

"To do what with clothes?"

"Hide my clothes there."

"Approximately where is this spot?"

"It's on the side of 834 West Agatite."

"Which side?"

"The left side."

"The left side as you are facing it?"

"Repeat that?"

"Where on the left side is this spot?"

"It's like in a courtway like."
"Did you hide the gun there?"
"No."
"Why not?"
"Because some clothes of mine came up stolen."
"What did you do then?"
"I then walked further down the alley, jumped this fence, and hid the gun in the corner of this building."
"Do you recall where that building is?"
"It is next to this parking lot."
"Which side of the parking lot is it on?"
"Like the middle, the part facing towards the alley."
"Where did you hide the gun?"
"In a corner on the side of this building in a plastic bag that I had in my pocket under some wood."
"How did you know to hide the gun there?"
"Because when I used to run away from Merryville, I hid my radio there?"
"After you hid the gun at that spot, what did you do then?
"I then climbed back over the fence, walked back down the alley, and went up to 854 West Agatite as to where Paul Phillips, Andrea Phillips, and Akia Phillips stayed."
"What was Baby T's assignment that night?"
"Look-out."
"What was Andrea Phillips's assignment that night?"
"Nothing."
"He wasn't involved?"
"She wasn't."
"Why did you go there?"
"Because when I ran away from ECS, they was my friends, and that is where I used to stay at."
"What did you guys do while you were there?"
"Smoked cigarettes, watched TV."
"Did later that night, did you go back to Oak Park, North Oak Park?"
"No, then the apartment got raided, and the apartment had got

raided once before so they found drugs in the house. And they took Andrea Phillips to jail and left Paul Phillips upstairs. At the time, Baby T was going over to his friend's house , and they brought me downstairs and asked me to show them where Baby T was. I then assisted them to Baby T."

"What happened then?"

"We went over to where Baby T was, and he was there, and then put him in a car, and they dropped me off at Merryville."

"Merryville is a shelter?"

"Yes."

"The spot aht you hid the gun, had the Vice Lords used that as a hiding spot before?"

"Yes."

"I am going to show you what has been marked as exhibit #1 and ask you to take a look at exhibit #1. Do you recognize that?"

"Yes."

"What is that?"

"The drawing of the area."

"The area of what?"

"Of where we planned to kill these guys, the guy and the lady."

"Now I am giving you a red pencil. On that map, I would like you to place a number where the meeting was, where you planned out what happened. And also on the map, if you could place a number two where lewis garner lookout spot was. Could you also place a number three on there to show Deon Phillips lookout post? Now could you place a number four on there where Paul Phillips look post was? Could you place a nu mber five on there where Slick's lookout post was? Now could you put a number six on the door where you, Rock, and Goldie weaned into the apartment? Now Daniel, I have what has been marked as exhibit #2 and ask you to take a look at that. Do you recognize exhibit #2?"

"Yes."

"What is that?"

"A picture of C Deon."

"I have what is exhibit #3 and ask you to take a look at that. Can you tell me who Exhibit #3 is?"

Conspired Confessions

"Picture of Paul Phillips."

"I have what is exhibit #4. Can you take a look at #4?"

"A picture of Akia Phillips known as Baby T."

"I have what has been marked exhibit #5. Can you take a look at that?"

"It's a picture of Daniel Taylor, which is me."

"I have exhibit #6 and ask you to take a look at that?"

"Picture of Goldie."

"I have what has been marked exhibit #7 and ask you to take a look at that?"

"Picture of Timothy Cobb, known as Rock."

"I have what has been marked as #8 and ask you to take a look at that?

"Picture of Cuzzo."

"What was his role in this?"

"He has no role."

"Now Daniel, how did you come down to the police station tonight?"

"They came and picked me up from MYS."

"What is MYS?"

"Methodist Youth Service."

"Is that a group home?"

"Yes."

"That is the address you gave us on North Oak Park Avenue?"

"Yes."

"Did you agree to come with the police down here tonight?"

"Yes."

"Now since you have been here, how have the police treated you here?"

"Fine.

"Have you been offered food to eat?"

"No, I was not hungry."

"Have you been offered anything to drink?"

"No."

"Have you been given any cigarettes?"

"Yes."

"Have you been allowed to use the bathroom?"
"Yes."
"Has anybody threatened you?"
"No."
"Has anybody promised you anything in return for your statement?"
"No."
"The court reporter will now type up your statement. We will then read over the entire statement to go over it, and you will be allowed to make any additions or corrections that you want. Do you understand that?"

The witness: "yes."

Mr. Magats: "This will conclude the statement of Daniel Taylor. The time is now 5:52 am."

But as Daniel sat there, a chilling realization settled over him. The responses he had given were one thing, but on paper, something entirely different was written. His words had been manipulated to fit the officers' narrative. The officers had twisted and reshaped his statements, ensuring they aligned perfectly with their version of events. Any mention of promises or coercion was conveniently glossed over or omitted. It was a masterful orchestration designed to elicit a false confession, and Daniel was just a pawn in their game.

The officers had repeated the same process with Rodney Mathews and Joseph Brown, hand-writing their statements to suit their story. Each statement was carefully crafted, strategically altered to build a false narrative. The officers meticulously ensured that every detail in these coerced confessions pointed towards a cover-up story, implicating seven young boys and men. The officers took full advantage of this. They used intimidation, threats, and deceit to shape his words into a confession that fit their needs. Each of them was up against a system that was determined to use him as a scapegoat.

With the statements from Daniel, Rodney, Paul, Lewis, Deon, Akia, and Joseph, the officers felt confident. They had created a cohesive story, a web of lies that implicated innocent young men. The officers' conspiracy was nearly complete, each fabricated confession a piece of the puzzle designed to protect their interests and cover up the truth. All of

Conspired Confessions

the young boys and men except Daniel ended up staying in jail until their trial date was set. As the time went by, the realization of this deceit marked a turning point in all of their lives. In March 1995, the trial dates were set and Deon and Lewis were the first to battle against the system in the courtroom.

Paul watched in helpless frustration as the prosecution took aim not only at him but also at his brother, Akia. What should have been a unified front in their defense had turned into a nightmare. Akia's cooperation with the authorities, something they'd hoped might mitigate the severity of their situation, was now being weaponized against them. Yet, despite the odds, Akia had managed to beat his case. His lawyer had filed a motion to suppress a statement and squash arrest that had been gathered through dubious means. It was a small victory in a fight that had seemed impossible to win, a moment where the truth had momentarily shone through the fog of deceit. But Paul's relief was short-lived. The same officers who had built their shaky case against Akia now turned their full attention to Paul. They weren't going to let another one slip through their fingers. With a vindictiveness that was palpable, they began pulling strings behind the scenes, manipulating the system to ensure Paul's conviction. Their tactics were ruthless.

Knowing their initial case against Paul was weak, they dug into his past and resurrected an old drug charge that had been buried for years. It was a case that had no relevance to the current charges, but they used it as a lever to exert pressure on both Paul and Akia. The message was clear: if Paul didn't plead guilty, they would make sure he paid dearly for it.

Paul's lawyer—whom he had trusted with his life—came back with a chilling message: "The judge knows me. We play golf together. I can get you a lighter sentence, but only if you cop out and take the deal." It was a conversation that blurred the lines between justice and personal favors, leaving Paul feeling more like a pawn than a man with a right to a fair trial.

"They're offering you 30 years," the lawyer said, his tone matter-of-fact, as if it was a simple negotiation over something trivial. Paul's heart sank. The idea of spending three decades behind bars for a crime he didn't commit was unbearable. His mind raced, thinking about the life he would lose—the family he would leave behind, the future he would never see. But his lawyer continued, trying to sweeten the deal. "If you take the 30 years, I can try to get it down to 20. You've already been in here for almost three years, which counts as six with day-for-day credit. You could be out in four years, back with your family."

Paul felt a cold knot form in his stomach. The deal sounded tempting on the surface, especially when faced with the possibility of spending decades behind bars. But he knew that accepting it would mean admitting to a crime he didn't commit, and that was something he couldn't do. It wasn't just about the time he would serve—it was about the principle, about holding onto his truth in a system that was trying to strip it away. The courtroom had become a battlefield, and Paul was caught in the crossfire. The officers who had failed to convict Akia were now hell-bent on ensuring that Paul didn't escape their grasp. They were using the old drug case as leverage, a way to force Paul into submission. But despite the overwhelming pressure, Paul refused to give in. He thought of Akia's victory, the motion to suppress that had saved him from a wrongful conviction. Paul knew that his situation was different, that the stakes were higher now. The prosecution was determined to make an example out of him, to prove that they could still wield their power, even if it meant bending the rules.

As the trial wore on, Paul's resolve hardened. He knew the odds were against him, knew that the courtroom had become a place where justice was a distant ideal rather than a guiding principle. But he also knew that he couldn't let fear dictate his actions. The deal offered by the prosecution might have seemed like a lifeline, but Paul saw it for what it was—a trap. But Paul knew better. He knew that taking the deal meant admitting to something he didn't do. It meant accepting guilt for a crime he had no part in. He looked at his lawyer, who seemed more interested in closing the case than fighting for his innocence, and a deep sense of betrayal settled over him.

"I'm not taking nothing," Paul said firmly, rejecting the plea deal that was being forced down his throat. His decision was a stand for the truth, but it came with a heavy price. The trial continued, and as it dragged on, Paul's hope began to wane. The real shock came when Paul was suddenly removed from Rock's case and placed with his brother

Conspired Confessions

Akia for a joint motion. It was a maneuver that left Paul bewildered and vulnerable.

The legal machinations surrounding everyone's case were rife with misconduct. Officers had collected photos of individuals from the neighborhood—people they often hung out with—and used these images to indiscriminately round up suspects without any probable cause. The nicknames and descriptions provided were so common in the community that there was no definitive way to identify the right people. The officers' decision to push forward without acknowledging Faye's testimony was not just an oversight; it was a deliberate act of malfeasance. They needed a conviction, and they were willing to sacrifice the truth to get it. This wasn't just about pinning a crime on someone; it was about maintaining control, about power. The officers had created a story, and now they were determined to see it through, no matter who got hurt in the process. And in the shadow of their ambition, young lives were being irreparably damaged. This lack of specificity and the officers' arbitrary methods further underscored the injustices at play. The entire process was a farce, designed more to secure convictions than to seek the truth.

Chapter 9

The Courtroom Conspiracy

As the trial loomed, the boys found themselves trapped in a nightmare, one that was meticulously constructed by those sworn to uphold justice. The reality of their situation was sinking in—there was no escape from the web of lies that had been spun around them. The courtroom was a sea of murmurs as Deon sat at the defense table, his heart pounding in his chest. His attorney's words faded into a distant hum, replaced by the gravity of the moment. The jury had returned, and their verdict was about to be read. Deon felt a cold sweat trickle down his back as he tried to steady his breathing. This was it—the moment that would determine his fate.

As the foreman stood and began to speak, the room fell into an eerie silence. Each word seemed to echo in Deon's mind, the reality of the situation crashing down on him with relentless force. "Guilty," the foreman announced, his voice reverberating in the courtroom. The words hit Deon like a sledgehammer, each syllable shattering his hopes and dreams. He had been found guilty of a crime he did not commit.

The possibility of facing the death penalty loomed over him like a dark cloud. Deon glanced at his family, their faces etched with shock and despair. He wanted to reassure them, to tell them he was okay, but he couldn't find the words. Inside, he felt a storm of emotions—fear, anger, and a deep, aching sadness. He tried to put on a brave face, not wanting them to worry about him, not wanting them to think he might harm himself. But the truth was, he wasn't okay.

That night, Deon sat with his Co-defendant (Rodney) and talked for hours. They spoke about the future, about hope, and about the fight that lay ahead. Deon tried to convince everyone that he was alright, that he could handle this. He wanted to ease their minds, to prevent them from fearing the worst. He had never thought of harming himself, but he knew the toll this was taking on his family. He needed to be strong for them, even if he felt anything but strong inside.

In the cold, stark confines of his cell, Deon struggled to keep his emotions in check. He knew that showing vulnerability could be dangerous, that he needed to project strength at all times. But the facade was exhausting. When he was alone, the weight of his circumstances pressed down on him, and he allowed himself to feel the despair that he hid from the world.

Deon was only 22, still a kid in many ways, grappling with the harsh realities of life. The thought of his children weighed heavily on him. How could he be a father from behind bars? How could he guide them, support them, when he was trapped in this nightmare? His mind raced with questions and fears, but he knew he had to keep fighting. For his family, for his children, for himself.

He thought back to his grandmother and her unwavering strength. Her words echoed in his mind, a source of comfort and inspiration. He told himself that they would figure this out, that they just had to fight harder than they had ever imagined. His family's belief in him was the motivation he needed to keep going.

The day of the verdict was a turning point. Hearing those words—"guilty"—was like a knife to the heart. But Deon dug deep, finding a reservoir of strength he didn't know he had. This was just the beginning of his battle. He resolved to fight with everything he had, to prove his innocence and reclaim his life.

As he lay in his cell that night, Deon felt a flicker of hope. The road ahead would be long and arduous, but he was determined to see it through. He would fight for his freedom, for his family, for his future. And no matter how dark the days became, he vowed to finish strong.

Lewis sat in the courtroom, a mixture of fear and confusion churning inside him. He didn't fully understand the gravity of the situation; his lawyer had done little to prepare him. From the few conversations they had, it was clear his attorney was not fighting for him. He hadn't explained the charges or what to expect in court. Lewis only knew he was on trial for murder, a concept that felt surreal and distant.

The trial began, and Lewis felt like a spectator at his own fate. He had no questions to ask, no strategy to follow. He just sat and listened, feeling more like a prop than a person. His lawyer had visited him once, briefly, and had mentioned he was being charged as a lookout. Lewis was baffled. Lookout for what? He had no idea what the crime even involved. He had repeatedly told his lawyer that he knew nothing about any murder, but his lawyer seemed indifferent.

Initially, the state had tried to charge Lewis as a juvenile. When that didn't work out, they charged him as an adult. He had been in the juvenile system since he was 15, and now at 17, he was being transferred to the county for a preliminary hearing. At that hearing, the charges were read out again, and Lewis was bewildered. He kept telling his lawyer he had no involvement, no knowledge of any murder, but it seemed no one was listening.

The days in court were long and grueling. Lewis was terrified, feeling utterly unprepared and alone. His lawyer's only advice was to stick to the statement he had previously given. But as Lewis took the stand, the truth clawed at him. He had lied in that statement under pressure and fear. Now, he was being asked to perpetuate that lie, to live with it hanging over him. The weight of those falsehoods pressed down on him, and he couldn't keep it up. He began to falter, contradicting the statement, and admitting, "No, I'm just lying. Why should I keep lying?"

His lawyer's incompetence became painfully apparent during the trial. There was no solid defense, no evidence presented on Lewis's behalf. The lawyer seemed content to let the prosecution shape the narrative. Lewis, sitting in the defendant's chair, felt like he was watching his life unravel. He didn't know the people involved in the

The Courtroom Conspiracy

case; he had no connection to the crime. Yet, here he was, facing the possibility of spending the rest of his life in prison.

One day, the reality of his situation hit him hard. His lawyer told him he could be facing up to 90 years or life in prison. The number was staggering, incomprehensible. Lewis was just a scared teenager, caught in a legal nightmare that felt like a bad dream. During the trial, he realized he was nothing more than a body in a chair, an easy target for a conviction.

After the trial sessions, Lewis was taken back to his cell. The conditions were harsh; he barely ate, and the nights were long and lonely. Sitting in the holding area, waiting for each court appearance, felt like an eternity. His mind raced with thoughts of his family, his lost freedom, and the bleak future that awaited him. He was overwhelmed with a sense of helplessness and fear.

When the judge asked if he had anything to say before sentencing, Lewis hesitated. His throat was dry, and his mind was a whirlwind of fear, anger, and desperation. But he knew he had to speak. He needed to say something, anything, that might make them see him as a human being, not just a statistic.

"I'm sorry for the family," Lewis finally said, his voice trembling but clear. He could see the pain in their faces, the raw grief that had been turned against him, and it broke something inside him. "You know, that said on the stand."

The prosecutor pounced on his words, not missing a beat. "Well, if you didn't do anything, why are you sorry?"

Lewis felt the sting of the question, the trap it was meant to be. But he wasn't sorry for what they accused him of. He was sorry because someone had lost their life, and that loss was real, no matter who was to blame. "Because they're human beings," he replied, meeting the prosecutor's eyes with a look of defiance. "Somebody got killed." As soon as the words left his mouth, Lewis felt a wave of resignation wash over him. He knew then that it was over. In their eyes, his apology was an admission of guilt, not the expression of empathy that he had intended.

As the trial progressed, Lewis's despair grew. He felt abandoned by the system, his lawyer, and even by fate. He had no control over the proceedings, no way to influence the outcome. The prosecution's story painted him as a criminal, but he knew the truth. He was innocent, a young man trapped in a web of lies and legal maneuvering.

The trial was a devastating experience for Lewis. The lack of preparation, the pressure to lie, and the overwhelming sense of injustice left him broken and disillusioned. He realized that in the eyes of the court, he was just another case to be processed, another conviction to be secured. As the final days of the trial approached, Lewis knew he had to find a way to keep fighting, to hold on to the hope that somehow, the truth would come to light.

Paul never imagined that the pursuit of justice would turn into a nightmare. The trial was meant to be his chance to prove his innocence, but as the days wore on, it became clear that the system was not in his favor. It all began when he found himself in the courtroom, seated next to Rodney Matthews—better known as "Rock"—as they both faced a barrage of accusations.

July 13th arrived, bringing with it the day of reckoning. Paul sat in the courtroom, listening as the charges were read out—30 years for attempted murder, 30 years for home invasion, and 30 years for armed robbery. The sentences ran concurrently, a small mercy in a storm of injustice. As the judge spoke, the words seemed to blur, the weight of the moment crushing Paul's spirit.

"30 years..." The number echoed in his mind, louder than anything else in the room. He could barely hear what was being said; all he could think about was his age, and how this sentence would consume the prime of his life. The realization hit him like a freight train—he would be an old man by the time he was free, if he survived that long.

The courtroom, once a symbol of law, now felt like a prison. Paul's world was spinning out of control, everything around him fading into a dull roar. The judge's voice was just noise, the faces in the courtroom a blur. All he could think about was how he would survive the next 30 years in a place where violence was the norm and hope was a rare commodity.

After the verdict, Paul wanted nothing more than to see his family, to hold onto the people who mattered most. But the system, in its cold efficiency, denied him even that small comfort. He was whisked away, not even allowed a moment with his mother before he was taken back to the holding cell. The cold steel bars closed behind him, a grim reminder of the years ahead.

Paul sat in the silence of the cell, his mind racing with thoughts of survival. He had heard the stories—how life inside was brutal, how fights and stabbings were routine. He wondered how he would endure, how he would protect himself in a place where humanity seemed to be left at the door. The fear of the unknown gnawed at him, but so did the determination to survive, to one day walk out of this nightmare with his dignity intact. In the end, the trial wasn't just about guilt or innocence; it was about survival. And as Paul prepared for the long years ahead, he knew that the fight for his life had only just begun. The courtroom had been the first battleground, but now he was stepping into a world where the stakes were even higher, where every day would be a battle for his very existence.

Daniel sat in the courtroom, feeling the weight of every decision that had brought him to this moment. The room was stifling, the air thick with the tension of a trial that had already drained him of so much. His thoughts kept circling back to a single question: How had it come to this?

There was a time when hope had felt within reach, when Attorney Kathleen Zellner, known for her fierce dedication to her clients, had seemed like the beacon of light they all needed. But that hope dimmed quickly when it became clear that Zellner wasn't willing to represent the entire group of wrongfully accused men. She wanted to pick and choose, and Daniel couldn't accept that. In his mind, they had all gone in together, and they needed to come out together. If Zellner wouldn't represent him and Deon, then he wouldn't accept her help at all.

"We didn't do this," Daniel kept telling himself, as if the repetition might somehow change the outcome. But he knew the truth was more complicated than that. The legal system they were up against was a juggernaut, one that had already consumed the lives of so many around him.

Lewis Gardner and Paul Phillips, along with Deon and Daniel, were still locked up, while others like Rodney Matthews, Akia Phillips, and

Joseph Brown had managed to escape the clutches of this broken system. Akia had won his freedom when the court acknowledged the coercion behind his confession—officers had promised him that if he gave a statement, he'd be able to go home. That single lie had unraveled the case against him. But Daniel wasn't so lucky. His statement didn't have that same loophole, and so he remained trapped.

Chapter 10

Reality Sets In

The prison walls weren't just physical barriers; they were constant reminders of everything Daniel, Deon, Paul, and Lewis had lost and the harsh reality of who they were forced to become. Thrust into the brutal environment of Cook County Jail as young adults, they quickly realized they weren't just surrounded by criminals—they were living among survivors, hardened men who had endured years of brutality and violence. These men weren't like that when they first walked through those gates. They weren't predators or power-hungry fighters, but prison had a way of reshaping people into someone they no longer recognized.

Over the first decade behind bars, the relentless environment slowly chipped away at their former selves. The years took a toll, hardening them on the outside while the hope that once sustained them began to fade. Each passing year made it harder to hold on to the person they once were, as despair crept in and the thought of spending a lifetime behind bars for something they didn't do became unbearable.

They often thought of the few men who had managed to walk free, even if only briefly. It gave them something to cling to, but as days turned into months and months into years, the flicker of hope grew dimmer. In the courtroom, it felt like justice was lost in a system more concerned with winning than truth. But even in the face of overwhelming odds, they knew they couldn't afford to give up—not when so much was still at stake.

Deon Patrick: The Struggle to Be Heard

My first week in prison felt like stepping onto a stage, where the script demanded I play a role that wasn't truly mine. Freshly convicted for a crime I didn't commit, I realized quickly that in a place like this, showing vulnerability was a luxury I couldn't afford. "You have to pretend," I told myself. "Pretend everything's fine, pretend nothing's wrong."

Every day, I kept up the facade, trying to carry on as if nothing had changed. Outside my cell, I put on a mask, projecting confidence and calm, knowing that in the brutal world of prison, any sign of weakness could be exploited. I saw the other men around me—some hardened by decades inside, some new like me, all navigating their own silent battles. The older ones had long ago learned to hide their emotions, becoming as tough as the walls that held them.

But when I returned to my cell, the mask came off. Alone, with no one watching, the weight of my situation crushed me. The walls I'd built up around myself outside dissolved, and I allowed myself to feel the fear, the anger, and the overwhelming sense of injustice. But I knew I couldn't let that show; not out there. If I did, it would be like bleeding in shark-infested waters.

My first year behind bars was a blur of anxiety and survival. They'd sent me three hours away from my family, and in the chaos of the Illinois Department of Corrections, danger was a constant companion. I avoided the law library for two and a half years, not because I didn't care about my case, but because my immediate focus was on staying alive. The environment was hostile, filled with men of all ages, many of whom had developed their own twisted methods of coping with the endless time stretching before them. Some had succumbed to the prison's perverse culture, engaging in activities my generation would never consider normal.

The reality of prison life hit me hard on my first day at Pontiac in

Reality Sets In

1995, one of the most notorious prisons in Illinois. Within hours of arriving, I witnessed six people being stabbed in the chapel. The violence was a brutal wake-up call, a stark reminder that I needed to be on high alert at all times. The penitentiary was a world where the young and inexperienced, like me, had to learn quickly or suffer the consequences. I knew then that my life depended on my ability to adapt quickly and protect myself at all costs.

In the midst of the chaos, my journey became one of finding a balance between the daily need to survive and the long-term battle to prove my innocence. Each day was a test, a battle between the man I had to pretend to be outside of this cell and the man I really was inside it. I found myself caught in a desperate cycle of trying to make someone—anyone—listen to the truth. I took advice from other inmates, guys who had been in the system longer than I had, and who claimed to know the ins and outs of how to get back into court. Their advice led me down a path that, looking back, was filled with missteps. I started filing affidavits and making claims that weren't entirely accurate. It wasn't that I was lying—I was just in a mode of desperation, trying to push the needle enough to make a judge pay attention.

For two years, I lived in survival mode, doing everything I could to avoid trouble and stay out of harm's way. I was surrounded by men who had spent decades in prison, some of whom had developed twisted ways of coping with their time behind bars. These men had become hardened by years of incarceration, and their behavior often shocked and repulsed me. But I couldn't afford to be repulsed. I had to navigate this world, find my footing, and ensure no one saw me as an easy target. Despite the challenges, I found a way to connect with a few inmates who, like me, were trying to maintain a semblance of humanity in a dehumanizing environment. These bonds were rare, but they were a lifeline, providing a small measure of support in a place where empathy was in short supply.

It wasn't until after a tragic incident—where a fellow inmate was killed by the prison guards—that I began to shift my focus. A fight had broken out between two gangs, and in the chaos, a guard had shot and killed an inmate. This death triggered a massive crackdown by the prison authorities, who feared retaliation. The yard, once filled with

The Hazel Boyz

hundreds of inmates, was now limited to small groups of fifty. With the violence contained, I found a sliver of mental space to begin working on my legal defense again. I began to frequent the law library, seeking ways to prove my innocence.

The truth, as I saw it, was getting buried under the weight of the system's indifference. We were telling our story, a story that was true at its core, but no one was listening. I became more focused on getting our voices heard than on the accuracy of the details. For instance, I might have said that I saw Daniel get arrested when, in fact, I hadn't witnessed it myself—I'd only heard about it later. But the point wasn't the specifics; it was that Daniel had been wrongfully taken away, and I needed people to understand that.

Years later, those small inaccuracies began to pile up. The timelines in my stories didn't always add up, and I started to feel the weight of that. But at the time, it didn't matter as much to me. What mattered was breaking through the silence that surrounded us, the silence that allowed injustice to fester. I knew that if I could just get someone to listen, the details could be sorted out later.

In 1997, my situation changed drastically. I was shipped out of Pontiac and sent to Menard. Within 20 days, I got into a fight and was thrown into segregation. That's when I had my wake-up call. Sitting in that cell, I realized that I couldn't keep going the way I was. I had to stop focusing on the short-term tactics and start thinking about the long game. When I got back to my unit in 1998, I made a commitment to myself to stay out of trouble, and for the most part, I did. I got put under investigation once for something I didn't do, but that was it.

My son came to visit me during that time. I remember how he fixated on the belt I was wearing, one of those belts with handcuffs attached that went through the belt loops. It broke my heart to see how fascinated he was with that belt because that's what his attention was drawn to, not to me, his father, but to the symbols of my captivity. After that visit, I told his mother not to bring him back while I was cuffed up. I didn't want him to see me like that anymore.

In 1998, I ended up at Statesville, which was only about 45 minutes from home. I stayed there for 12 years, mostly trouble-free, until an incident occurred that had nothing to do with me but ended up affecting

Reality Sets In

my life in a big way. I was working as a porter in the prison hospital, cleaning the cells of inmates who couldn't take care of themselves anymore. Some of those guys were in bad shape, sick and dying, and it was our job to make sure they were taken care of.

When I first started at the hospital, it was a shock. I had to clean up after men who were lying in their own filth, who hadn't been bathed in days, sometimes weeks. It was hard work, but it was also eye-opening. A friend of mine,(Al Dye) who had been there longer, told me that I needed to approach the job with compassion. He said, "You gotta have a humanitarian mindset. These nurses aren't doing their jobs, so if we don't help, these guys will just lay here and suffer."

He was right. We took on the responsibility because we knew it could easily be us one day, lying in one of those cells, needing someone to care. We couldn't just stand by and watch our fellow inmates suffer. We had to help, even when it wasn't easy.

In 2010, my work at the hospital was interrupted by a shakedown. They found $100 in cash in the inmate area and assumed it was mine. Internal Affairs took me in for questioning, but I told them straight up that it wasn't my job to play the police. I didn't know whose money it was, and I didn't care. But they had already made up their minds that it was mine. They couldn't prove it, though, so I never got any disciplinary time for it. Instead, they kept me under investigation for 30 days and then transferred me out of Statesville.

Going back to 1999, I'd been assigned my first job as a porter in the cell house, where I cleaned the gallery and picked up trash. At first, I didn't want a job. I'd just arrived in the penitentiary in 1995, and I wasn't interested in anything but surviving. But over the next few years, I realized that having a job was a way to take care of my business. It got me out of my cell, allowed me to help other inmates, and gave me more access to the law library. Being stuck in a cell 23 hours a day was no way to live. Working as a porter was a way to stretch my legs and feel a little bit human.

By 2007, I'd moved from working in the cell house to working in the hospital. The transition wasn't easy, but it taught me a lot about myself and about what it means to care for others, even in the most difficult circumstances.

During those years, my legal battles continued. My direct appeals were denied, and I filed a post-conviction petition. Around the same time, Daniel's appeal was also denied. We were both feeling the weight of the system pressing down on us, but we refused to give up.

It was in 1999 that we caught a break. Daniel's attorney, Deborah Finch, was devastated when his appeal was denied. She knew something had gone wrong in our case, just like every other attorney we'd encountered. She didn't have many options left, but she did have a friend who worked at the Chicago Tribune. She reached out to him, hoping he might take an interest in our story.

That's when we met Steve Mills, a reporter with the Tribune. He came to see us, and from the moment he sat down with us, I could tell he was different. He wasn't just going through the motions; he was genuinely interested in our story. He started taking notes, digging into the details, and asking the tough questions. For the first time, it felt like someone was truly listening.

Steve's first article about us came out in 2001, and it was the beginning of a series on false confessions, police corruption, and wrongful convictions in Chicago. He made sure our story was included in every part of that series, shining a light on the injustices we were facing.

Looking back, I realize how lucky we were to have someone like Steve in our corner. Most people in our situation never get that kind of media attention. But Steve saw something in our case that others had overlooked, and he made it his mission to tell the world what was happening.

For Daniel and me, meeting Steve Mills was a turning point. His articles brought our case to the attention of people who could help, people who could make a difference. And in the end, that attention is what led to Daniel's release in 2013.

As I reflect on those years, I see a journey marked by struggle, desperation, and, ultimately, hope. It was a long and winding road, filled with obstacles and setbacks. But through it all, we kept pushing forward, kept fighting for our freedom, and kept believing that one day, someone would listen. And eventually, they did.

Reality Sets In

Lewis Gardner: Surviving Pontiac

Jail in the '90s was no joke. It was a brutal, unforgiving place where hope went to die. I had heard the stories, and now I was living one of them. But nothing could have prepared me for the reality of it. The isolation, the violence, the constant fear—it was like being trapped in a nightmare that never ended.

I had never been to jail before in my life. The fear that gripped me as I sat on that cold, hard bench, waiting to get processed, was unlike anything I had ever felt. Everything about the place was foreign and terrifying. The walls felt like they were closing in, the air thick with a stench that I could only describe as a mix of sweat, desperation, and drugs. I was in Pontiac, and it smelled like a bunch of fiends on drugs. This was my introduction to the world I was about to be thrust into.

I tried to stay calm, but it was impossible. My mind was racing, my heart pounding in my chest. The fear gnawed at me, and all I could think about was how I ended up here, accused of a crime I didn't commit. It didn't seem real. None of it did. The courtroom, the trial, the accusations—it all felt like some horrible nightmare that I couldn't wake up from.

As I sat there, trying to make sense of it all, my first glimpse of what life was going to be like came in the form of a fight breaking out in front of me. Two crackheads, their faces twisted with rage and desperation, went at each other like wild animals. The violence was sudden, brutal, and utterly terrifying. I just froze. I couldn't move, couldn't speak. I just sat still, paralyzed by fear, watching as they tore into each other. Man, I was in with the big boys. The real deal. In there, you either fought, got beat up, or joined a gang. You didn't have a choice. You had to play the game, whether you wanted to or not. I was one of the youngest on my block, barely 18, and a lot of the older guys looked out for me. Some tried to guide me the right way, while others were still deep in the life, carrying knives and all that, because that's what you had to do to survive. There was no getting out of it. If you didn't do it, you'd be the one getting hurt.

One of my first memories in Pontiac was having to protect myself. I remember it clear as day. We were on the gallery when a fight broke out.

The Hazel Boyz

One of the guys got jumped, and the whole place erupted. Fights were common, but this one got out of hand, and someone ended up getting stabbed. Retaliation was immediate and brutal. I was on security duty that day, meaning I had to carry a knife. But no one had told me the unwritten rules, like how to ditch the knife if the cops showed up.

When the police came, one of the older guys yelled at me to get rid of the knife. I panicked, not knowing what to do. I threw the knife away, thinking that was the smart move, but that just put a target on my back. You either got caught with a weapon, or you didn't have one at all—those were the only two acceptable options. I learned quickly that making mistakes like that could cost you your life.

There was another time when things got real ugly. It was when Deon was down there with us. We were in the chapel, and a riot broke out. Someone got killed down in the cells, and chaos followed. We were all fighting, and it got so bad that the guards had to pull us out and lock us in the gym. The tension in that gym was thick. We were split into two sides, gangs on one, and those trying to stay out of trouble on the other. It could have gone bad real fast, but before anything popped off, the guards stormed in and broke it up. If they hadn't, it would've been a bloodbath.

I'll never forget the day my cellmate, an older guy who had seen it all, told me I needed to get out of Pontiac. He said this wasn't a place for someone like me. He helped get me transferred to Danville, which was a bit better, but I was still deep in that prison mentality. I'd get into fights over stupid things like a basketball game or a card dispute. But gradually, things started to change. I started working odd jobs in the prison, selling sandwiches on the gallery, or vegetables from the warehouse. It was a way to pass the time, but also a way to start thinking beyond the walls around me.

I got caught up in some trouble when I was working in the commissary. I was stealing tobacco, got caught, and ended up in solitary. Sitting there, all by myself, I had a lot of time to think. I realized I wasn't doing anything with my life, just wasting away, caught in a cycle of violence and crime. That's when I decided to change. I enrolled in classes to get my GED and started cutting ties with the knuckleheads who kept pulling me back into that life. I began walking the yard more, working

Reality Sets In

out, playing basketball, and trying to find ways to keep my mind occupied with something other than surviving day to day.

Books became my escape. I read history books, novels, even tried to read the Bible once. But the most important lesson I learned wasn't from a book—it was that life is what you make of it. Nothing is guaranteed, and no one is going to hand you a better future. You have to decide to change, and then do the hard work to make it happen. By then, I'd been inside for 12 or 13 years. I watched as the prison atmosphere slowly started to shift, with more opportunities to better yourself if you were willing to take them.

I saw too many guys getting out, just to come right back in. They couldn't break free from the mentality that kept them trapped in the same cycle. But I was determined not to be that person. I knew I had to change, or I'd end up like them, stuck in a loop that led nowhere. I started associating with people who wanted to change, who were trying to do better. I even began talking to the guards, something I never thought I'd do. One guard in particular told me something that stuck with me. He said, "Why do you hate us so much? We're just here to do a job, to provide for our families. We're not your enemy." That hit me hard. It made me see things differently. I realized that holding onto hate was only hurting me.

So, I started to do more positive things. I kept reading, working out, and distancing myself from the gangs and the troublemakers. I knew I had to get out of that jail mentality if I wanted any chance at a life beyond these walls. It wasn't easy, but it was the only way forward.

I had to change. My life depended on it. And little by little, I did. Reading started to shift something in my perspective. The books taught me that life is not guaranteed, and it's not something that's handed to you on a silver platter. Life is what you make of it. That was a hard pill to swallow, especially for someone like me, who felt like life had taken everything from him. But the more I read, the more I realized that I had a choice. I could keep walking down the path I was on, filled with anger and resentment, or I could change it. It wasn't going to be easy, but staying the same wasn't doing me any good either. I was tired of going in circles, doing the same things over and over, expecting different results. It took me years to see it, but I finally did.

The Hazel Boyz

Around that time, I noticed something different in the air. The atmosphere in the jail started to shift. It was like the powers that be decided to make things better for the people who actually wanted to change. For those of us who were tired of the same old cycle. I didn't want to be that guy who we all saw coming in and out of jail, never learning, never growing. Jail, as hard as it was, had a way of showing you who you really were. If you weren't doing anything in here, you sure as hell weren't doing anything out there in the free world.

I remember this one guy—he came back to jail five times during my sentence. Five times! Watching him, I realized I didn't want that to be me. I couldn't let that be me. So, I started making changes. I began to distance myself from the knuckleheads, the ones who were always getting into trouble, always up to no good. I started hanging around different people, people who wanted more out of life, even if we were stuck in a place like this. It was a small thing, but it made a world of difference. You hang with trouble, you find trouble. But you hang with those who are trying to better themselves, and you start doing the same.

And then, something surprising happened—I started talking to the officers more. At first, I hated them. They were the face of the system that had put me in here, the system that had wronged me. But one day, one of the officers asked me, "Why do you hate me so much?"

I didn't know what to say at first. "What you mean?" I asked him.

"Why do you hate me so much?" he repeated.

"Because you're the police," I said, like it was the most obvious thing in the world.

He looked at me for a moment and then said, "I'm not the police. I'm a human being and a correctional officer."

That hit me. I realized then that I had been so blinded by my anger that I hadn't seen the person standing in front of me. He wasn't just an officer; he was a man doing a job, just like I was a man trying to survive in here. We were both human, and that realization changed everything.

I started seeing the officers differently after that. Not as enemies, but as people. Some of them were just as stuck in this place as we were, trying to make it through their shifts just like we were trying to make it through our sentences. That understanding didn't make the walls disappear, but it made them feel less suffocating. The changes I made in myself didn't happen overnight, and they weren't easy. But they were necessary. I didn't want to be that guy who kept coming back, who never learned, who never grew. I wanted more. I deserved more. And so, I made the choice to change. I stopped doing the same things over and over, stopped hanging with the wrong crowd, and started focusing on what I could control—myself.

Paul Phillips: The Weight of Injustice

When the judge's gavel came down, declaring me guilty, it felt like the world had closed in around me. It wasn't just the sound of that wooden mallet echoing through the courtroom—it was the heavy silence that followed, the kind that presses down on your chest and makes it hard to breathe. I didn't cry, I didn't flinch, but inside, everything was crumbling.

After the verdict, they gave me a few moments with my family before they took me away. I remember walking into the room where my mom, grandmother, and a few others were waiting. The air was thick with sorrow, like everyone knew it was the last time we'd be together like that. My mom didn't say much. She just looked at me, her eyes full of pain that she couldn't put into words. My grandmother, though, kept saying that I should have gone to trial, that I should have fought harder. But I had trusted my lawyer when he told me to take the plea, and I had prayed, asking God to guide me. I thought I was doing the right thing, but standing there, seeing the hurt in their faces, I wasn't so sure anymore.

They told me they loved me, that they'd be there for me, but my mom just stared, her silence louder than anything else in that room. I wanted to hold onto her, to hold onto all of them, but I knew that time was up. As I turned to walk away, it was like leaving everything I knew behind—like stepping into a void.

When they led me to the back, the reality of it all started to sink in. I wasn't just walking away from my family; I was walking into a new life —a life behind bars. My mind was racing. I kept thinking about what prison would be like, imagining all the things I'd seen in movies, trying

The Hazel Boyz

to prepare myself for the worst. But no amount of preparation could really get you ready for that.

It's like you have to strip away everything you love, everything that makes you human, and put on this armor just to survive. As I walked, I tried to shut down my emotions, to focus on what was coming next. Survival became my only goal. I couldn't afford to think about the life I was leaving behind because that life was gone. My world had been reduced to this moment, this walk, this new reality.

The first week in prison was a blur. They placed me on a deck with younger inmates, and it was chaos. There was a lot of playing around, but underneath it, there was this underlying tension, this unspoken understanding that we were all just trying to figure out how to get through each day. They say you're innocent until proven guilty, but inside those walls, it feels like you're guilty until proven innocent—if that ever happens.

I didn't know anyone, didn't know the rules or how things worked there. I spent most of that first week just talking to my cousin, trying to get a handle on the situation. He'd been through it, and he gave me advice, told me what to expect. It helped, but it didn't make it any easier. Every day felt like a battle, and all I could think about was how to protect myself—and my brother.

We were tight on the streets, and we stuck together inside. But prison changes things. We were still close, but there was this pressure, this feeling that something was always trying to pull us apart. They sent me to different parts of the prison, separating us, trying to break us down. I ended up on a deck with older inmates, and in some ways, it was easier—there wasn't as much drama. But my brother was struggling. He never adapted, never understood that this was life now. It was like he was a deer in front of lions, and I couldn't protect him. That weighed on me every day.

My first year in prison was all about survival. I learned the rules, figured out who to trust, and kept my head down. But I never stopped thinking about my innocence. I always knew I had to prove it, but I didn't know how. It wasn't until I started digging into my case, going to the law library, and talking to other inmates who knew the system, that I realized my lawyer hadn't even filed an appeal. That's when the pieces started to fall into place.

I started to see that my lawyer wasn't just incompetent—he was connected to the police, the same police who had wronged me when I was a kid. It all started to make sense, how he had pushed me into a plea, how he had ignored the witnesses I told him about, how he had taken my money and done nothing. The system wasn't just broken—it was rigged against me from the start.

That's when I knew I had to fight. I couldn't just sit back and let this happen. I had to prove my innocence, not just for me, but for my family, for everyone who had been hurt by this. But it wasn't easy. The system wasn't built for people like me to win. Appeals were denied, motions ignored, but I kept going. I had to. I couldn't let them win.

That first year changed me. It stripped away everything I thought I knew and left me with nothing but my will to survive and my determination to prove the truth. It was a fight every day, but it was a fight I was ready for.

Spiritual Notes from Paul titled "Pain"

"That's why this pain runs deep.
This pain that I feel goes deep into my soul.
I didn't feel this as a kid.
I felt this pain when I got old.
I'm tired of people looking at my situation, you out like I never had a separation
the preparation God put me in was isolation and segregation.
This manifestation is my dedication.
You said you feel sorry for what I've been through. You said you got a lot of admiration.
All I'm trying to do is be a blessing to you. I'm saying God made your struggles my obligation.
See, I know you're going through a lot of storms and trials in this generation, but since God put me in a place of elevation
doesn't mean I Paul doesn't have the same tribulations.
I'm telling you, everybody goes through storms and trials

from Genesis always to Revelations.
But let's go back in time.
I'm saying just let everybody rewind.
I'm talking about the late 80s, early 90s, 2000 and all y'all were fine.
I was locked up doing hard time.
I never said this journey wasn't mine.
Y'all was out here enjoying life, eating good, laughing and living fine.
But now, since y'all going through what y'all going through, comparing y'all life to mine,
I never compare my life to anyone, because whatever state I'm in, I'm fine.
I understand right now I look alive.
But it was a time when I was walking through this world.
I'm telling y'all, man, I was dying.
My heart was crying.
I'm locked up in prison. I'm complying.
I write letters to people I love.
No one's replying.
I call collect. I'm not lying,
I have no answers, Im trying
Would you accept this collect call
they told me, No. They denying
Y'all in the streets, living life.
I'm in jail steady dying,
your birthday come with surprises.
My birthday comes with surviving.
You cut your cake with your knife.
You gonna get a whole lot of
I'm seeing knives up inside of people
I'm standing beside of."

Daniel Taylor: Fighting Against the System

Once I was convicted, I was sent to prison. I was 19 years old, and my life as I knew it was over. From that moment, I began the long, painful process of fighting for my freedom. I started my appeal process right away, but every appeal I filed was denied. My direct appeal, the one that

Reality Sets In

was supposed to be the most straightforward, was not even reconsidered. It was just denied. Then I filed a post-conviction petition. Denied. I appealed the denial of my post-conviction petition and was denied again. It felt like a never-ending cycle of rejection. I started to feel lost, like I was trapped in a nightmare that I couldn't wake up from. But I knew I couldn't give up. I had to prove that I didn't do it. I knew the police had evidence that could clear me, but I just couldn't get to it.

At some point during the appeals process, I realized that I had to start filing the appeals myself. Here I was, not educated enough to defend myself properly, but with no other choice. After your direct appeal, everything—every motion or petition that you file at different stages—you have to do it yourself. So I had to learn how to file a petition, how to put it in legal format, and how to look up case law to argue the different points where I believed my rights were violated. It was a process. I got some help from what people on the inside call "jailhouse lawyers." These were guys who helped me understand the law, how to read it, how to write it, and how to put it into the correct format. They helped me file my appeals and fight this case.

But at every turn, the answer was always the same: deny, deny, deny. They denied my appeal in the early 2000s. Around that time, a story was published about my case, and I was writing letters to attorneys, trying desperately to get legal representation. Eventually, I got a response from Kathleen Zellner. When she took over my case, I was already deep into the appeal of my post-conviction denial. Of course, I was excited. My spirits lifted a bit because I finally had an actual attorney who could help me prove my innocence.

But it turned out to be nothing. She came on the case, threw out my appeal, and I thought it was because she was going to file a brand new one. But she didn't. What she did was throw out my appeal to the denial of my post-conviction and then try to supplement it—unknown to me at the time. When you have something thrown out, it's thrown out, it's no longer valid. You can't supplement something that doesn't exist anymore. So the judges denied the appeal she put in front of them because of that. Then we tried to file another appeal from scratch. That too was denied.

One of the reasons, I believe, was because of something the judge said. She didn't believe that Nathan Diamond, my public defender at the time, would call himself a moron. But there was a newspaper article where the reporter quoted Nathan saying, "Why didn't I get this? I must have been a moron." But the judge didn't believe it. She didn't think he would say that about himself, and she denied my appeal. This was at the post-conviction level, so I had to go to the next stage, the Supreme Court.

I filed all my appeals based on actual innocence. My case wasn't one of those where there was DNA evidence or witnesses who identified me. There were no fingerprints tying me to the crime—nobody's fingerprints matched. When I got to the Supreme Court, I filed my petition, but they denied it too. So, I went to the federal habeas corpus and filed under actual innocence again. I was desperate, writing letters to the judge, which was the wrong thing to do, but I was just trying to express that I didn't do this. The judge told me I had to put the petition in legal format, so I did, and I continued the process of appealing in the federal courts.

But then, something happened that broke me. Kathleen Zellner sent me a letter saying that she wished me the best in my quest for freedom and that she was sorry things didn't work out between us. When I read that letter, I felt lost again. Now I was back to having no attorney, and I had to do everything myself. Mind you, during this time, I was still learning. I didn't have everything down pat, and I didn't know all the ins and outs of filing petitions. But I knew I had to keep trying. So I kept filing, trying to get things moving.

Eventually, I reached out to Northwestern University's Center on Wrongful Convictions. I sent them a letter explaining how I was innocent, why I was innocent, and how I was set up. They wrote back saying they were interested in my case but needed more information. They needed to come see me and talk to me. So we did that. They didn't take my case immediately because they take cases pro bono, so it took some time.

Karen Daniel, may she rest in peace, was the one who came to see me. She was a small woman, about five feet tall, but she had a powerful presence. In the courtroom, you could feel her strength radiating from her. She was a force to be reckoned with. She came to visit me about three different times before they actually accepted my case. I had to explain everything, go over all the details, and they did their own investigation. They gathered all the legal documents that had been filed in my case. I believe that's when they made the decision because anyone who reads that paperwork can clearly see that I should have never been convicted or sent to jail. Period. Never convicted, never sent to prison.

When she finally told me that they were going to take my case and represent me, I was over the moon. I was so happy, even though she kept reminding me that just because they were taking the case didn't mean I would get out. It just meant that they believed in my innocence and would do everything in their power to prove it. That meant the world to me. There was also a reporter, Steve Mills, who wrote about my case. He told me that he believed I was innocent too. Those two moments, when Karen and Steve told me they believed in my innocence, were powerful for me. For the first time, I had someone who wasn't a friend or family member saying they believed in me.

Karen Daniel represented me from 2008 to 2013. We had our ups and downs. But three weeks after I was first sent to prison, something happened that I haven't really shared in many interviews. I tried to take my own life.

I wasn't one of those people who just talked about it. I really meant to end it. One night, they passed out shaving razors. I took the blade out and slit my wrist. I just laid there, hoping to bleed out, to escape this hell. I thought I would just fade away, but obviously, that didn't happen. The guy in the cell next to me noticed the blood. I lost so much that it leaked through the mattress onto the floor. He saw it and called the guards.

They rushed me to the hospital, stitched me up, and then put me in a padded room for observation for three days. On the third day, they released me from observation and put me back in the same cell where I had tried to kill myself.

I was in Joliet prison for about three weeks when it all became too much. I looked at those steel bars, thinking about the rest of my life, and I cracked. I didn't do this crime, but they were going to keep me in prison forever. That night, I just lost it. I tried to end my life because I couldn't see any other way out.

Chapter 11

A Break In The Clouds

December 2001 was a time of intense desperation and tentative hope for the convicted men entangled in the unforgiving grasp of the prison system. While Daniel and Deon were locked within the walls of Stateville Correctional Center, a maximum-security penitentiary, Lewis was in Danville, and Paul was in Galesburg. Yet, despite our scattered locations, only Daniel and Deon were fully immersed in the unfolding media coverage that would later prove to be the first flicker of hope in their long, dark journey toward freedom.

As the years passed, Lewis and Paul focused on surviving the day-to-day grind of prison life, holding onto the certainty that freedom was on the horizon. They kept their heads down, maintaining jobs and preparing for the moment they would finally reunite with their families. But for Daniel and Deon, the fight was far from over. They became the voices of the forgotten, reaching out to the outside world in a desperate bid for justice.

The Chicago Tribune began to take notice. Reporters like Steve Mills were drawn to the glaring inconsistencies and injustices in their cases, leading to a series of articles that would slowly begin to unravel the truth. These articles, however, were not just the result of journalistic curiosity. They were carefully crafted with the help of Daniel and Deon, who provided crucial information from behind bars. They had become active participants in their own fight for freedom, even as they remained physically confined.

For Lewis and Paul, these articles were distant echoes of a battle they were no longer directly involved in. They had resigned themselves to the fact that their release would come with time, not through the media's intervention. It wasn't until they were home, reuniting with their loved ones, that they began to fully grasp the magnitude of what Daniel and Deon had been fighting for. They learned of the relentless efforts to expose the truth, efforts that had continued long after they had set their minds to simply enduring their sentences.

As the stories unfolded in the pages of the Tribune, they served as both a beacon of hope and a grim reminder of the uphill battle that remained. For Daniel and Deon, each article was a lifeline, a small step toward the justice they sought. Their collaboration with the journalists was not just about telling their story; it was about reclaiming their lives. This chapter delves into the impact of those early articles, the role they played in the fight for freedom, and the complex emotions that came with seeing their lives laid bare in the public eye.

Daniel's Thoughts

In 1999, I hit rock bottom. My direct appeal was denied, and I found myself alone, without an attorney, and with no clear direction on where to go next. I felt like I was sinking into a black hole of despair. The court's decision left me feeling hopeless, like I was shouting into an empty void where no one could hear me or cared to listen.

I didn't know what to file next or who could help me. For months, I felt paralyzed by fear and uncertainty. I remember thinking that maybe this was it. Maybe this was how my life would be—locked away for something I didn't do, with no chance of proving my innocence. But something inside me refused to let go.

One day, while sitting in my cell, I thought about reaching out to a news reporter. I had no idea if it would make a difference, but I was desperate. I needed someone, anyone, to listen to me, to hear my side of the story. So, I took a chance and got in touch with a reporter named Steve Mills.

When we met, I wasn't sure what to expect. Would he believe me? Would he care? We spent hours talking about my case, going over every detail, every piece of evidence, and every injustice. Steve listened intently, his face a mask of concentration as I poured out my heart. At the end of our meeting, he looked me in the eye and said, "Don't give up, Daniel. I'm by your side, and I'm not going anywhere until you're proven innocent."

Those words hit me like a wave. I had been drowning in despair, but here was someone offering me a lifeline. Steve Mills wasn't just a reporter; he became a friend, a confidant, someone who believed in me when no one else did. For the first time in a long time, I felt a spark of hope. Now with Steve Mills came on board, it felt like a massive weight had been lifted off my shoulders. Until that moment, I'd been fighting a relentless battle with little hope of winning. I was staring down the barrel of life sentences—two consecutive 30-year terms. As a young man with only a rudimentary understanding of the law, I was lost. I could read, write, and do arithmetic, but the law? That was a different beast entirely.

When he promised that he wasn't going anywhere until my innocence was proven, it was the first time I'd felt someone truly believed in my fight. He urged me to prepare myself, and that's when I knew I had to step up my game. I dove into a rigorous study routine, determined to equip myself with the knowledge I lacked. I began by copying the dictionary, front and back. It was a Herculean task, but I meticulously transcribed every page, both of the two sections that contained 1,000 pages each. I made it my mission to understand every word, every nuance. It was a painstaking process, but I knew it was crucial if I wanted to comprehend the legal jargon that had been a constant barrier in my previous court appearances.

Before Steve, my experience in court had been disheartening. I often found myself doodling aimlessly during proceedings because I couldn't grasp what was being said. Simple phrases like "I tender the fact that this is an expert witness" went over my head—like when they referred to the person as *tender* and I wondered why they called the dude "soft." In actuality, the phrase meant this person was an expert in their field. This was an indicator of how little I understood the legal world. I remember a time when I was called "facetious" by another inmate, and I had no clue what it meant. When I finally learned it meant I was either exaggerating or hiding something, I was embarrassed and motivated to improve.

My thirst for knowledge led me to become a teacher's aide after I earned my GED. I spent about seven to eight years helping others achieve their educational goals before losing that position. During that time, I also had to learn how to defend myself. I started filing petitions and writing legal documents, often stumbling through the process. I remember writing a letter to a judge that resembled a casual note rather than a formal legal document. Thankfully, the judge gave me a second chance, and his words—that ignorance of the law was no defense—hit me hard. He could have easily dismissed my appeal, but instead, he gave me a three-month extension to get my act together.

That three-month period was a turning point. I threw myself into studying legal books and learning from those who had become adept at navigating the system. Melvin Wilson, a fellow inmate who had become something of a "jailhouse lawyer," played a crucial role in this phase. He taught me how to look up and understand case law and how to apply it effectively. His guidance was invaluable. It wasn't just about knowing the law but using that knowledge to fight for my rights.

Steve Mills and Melvin Wilson gave me a fighting chance. They helped transform me from a man who was bewildered by legal jargon into someone who could actively engage in his own defense. Their support was more than just a lifeline; it was the foundation upon which I began to build my path to justice.

We worked together for months, piecing together my story, digging up the truth, and exposing the lies that had led to my conviction. On December 19, 2001, the first article in a series called "Cops and Confessions" was published by the Chicago Tribune. It detailed how police in Chicago coerced confessions from innocent people, using threats, manipulation, and illegal tactics. It was a powerful piece of journalism, shining a light on the dark corners of the justice system that had swallowed me whole.

CHICAGO TRIBUNE: *New doubts about confessions*
By: Steve Mills
December 19, 2001

The mind is a malleable thing, open to suggestion, prone to fatigue. Strength of will and confidence in one's own sense of reality can twist and bend. Most of us have a breaking point. And most of us would reach it after enduring several hours of threats, lack of sleep, manipulation and physical discomfort.

Smart police investigators know how to use that human vulnerability. Unscrupulous police investigators know how to abuse it.

In Chicago, such abuse is no rare thing.

After analyzing thousands of murder cases and appellate decisions, Tribune reporters Ken Armstrong, Steve Mills and Maurice Possley uncovered cases where people confessed to murders they didn't commit. The reporters found that some confessions were obtained using threats, coercion and illegal techniques. Some confessions, illustrated by today's tale of Daniel Taylor, were taken as gospel by police even when their own records suggested there was no way he could have committed the double murder.

Not surprisingly, most of the defendants who owned up to crimes they did not commit were either juveniles or adults with low intelligence, those most vulnerable to forceful persuasion.

"Cops and Confessions," the four-part series that concludes today, adds more evidence to one of Chicago's dirty secrets: Time and again, the innocent are tagged as guilty.

That's becoming less of a secret because of reporting such as this, and because advances in DNA technology more often provide evidence that someone who has confessed to a crime is not, in fact, guilty.

It starts with the way some police detectives approach murder cases: They focus their efforts on coercing tidy, efficient confessions rather than on exhausting all investigative leads.

This doesn't mean that the legal tactics police use to gain confessions should not be employed. It means they should be used with a judiciousness that pursues truth rather than simple closure. It means interrogations always should be com-plemented by skillful, aggressive police work and independent forensic analyses. They should be accompanied by stronger laws protecting juveniles who are questioned, rather than relying on parents and youth officers who can't al-ways be expected to have the legal knowledge to protect the child's rights.

The series also points, once again, to the need to document more comprehensively the custodial interrogations that lead up to confessions. They must be videotaped.

This won't solve all problems with questionable confessions, but it will clear up many. It also will help abbreviate and even eliminate many of the time-consuming pre-trial motions that come in attempts to suppress confessions.

A defendant claims his request to speak to an attorney early in the interrogation was ignored?

Go to the videotape.

A defendant claims that he was beaten with telephone books into confessing?

Go to the videotape.

Cook County State's Atty. Dick Devine has finally conceded that perhaps a pilot videotaping program of a limited num-ber of custodial murder interrogations should be started. Terrific. Why not start today? Murder confessions already are videotaped.

Unfortunately, the Chicago Police Department continues to resist. Why? Because it would involve a change of police culture.

Yes, it would. Good. Do it now.

Chicago police consistently have cited a litany of other reasons, too, including equipment cost, storage issues and the concern that juries would fail to understand certain tough interrogation tactics that police legally are allowed to use. For instance, police sometimes may lie to a suspect to help prompt his confession. But in Minnesota and Alaska, two states that already require videotaped interrogations, juries have shown an infinite capacity to understand such techniques.

What so many police departments around the country fail to under-stand about this issue is that when cops get lazy or sloppy and hammer away at extracting dubious confessions in lieu of more thorough investiga-tive work, the defendant isn't the only one victimized.

Family members of the murder victim are back to seeking justice long after they thought it was safe to move on. Chi-cago citizens remain unpro-tected from the real perpetrator of the crime, who has vastly increased his chances of getting away with murder. And investigators are stuck where they were months or years before, often long after the case has frozen over, witnesses have moved and memories have faded.

What remains is another black eye for law enforcement, one more reason for juries, judges and the public to doubt the integrity of police tactics and the veracity of their statements in court. Given what has been learned in recent years about casual mistakes made in the most serious of crimes, that is a new layer of doubt that law enforcement can ill afford.

New technology and videotaping, it should be noted, will go only so far in improving criminal justice. More hard work has to be done within the department itself. CPD still hasn't lived down its scandal involving Cmdr. Jon Burge, who eventually was fired for torturing a murder suspect. Then there was the notorious case of the 7- and 8-year-old boys who "confessed" to murdering 11-year-old Ryan Harris before forensic evidence implicated a convicted sex offender who has been charged with the crime.

The Chicago Police Department has many extraordinary officers, people who risk their lives for the city's citizens. The department does much fine work. But its silence on this issue has been so loud it hurts. Authorities have declined to respond to the Tribune investigation.

The agency is long overdue for serious soul-searching on its investigative techniques. That won't come without leader-ship from the likes of Supt. Terry Hillard and his lieutenants. The message has to be clear: The task of investigators is not just to close cases, but to solve them. Time and again, the innocent are tagged as guilty."

Daniel Continues

When I read that article, I felt something I hadn't felt in years—validation. Finally, someone was listening. Finally, someone believed my story. Someone was believing in me. Reading those words, I felt like a weight had been lifted off my shoulders. It was like I could breathe again for the first time since my nightmare began.

Hope surged through me, filling me with a newfound passion to keep fighting. I knew the road ahead would be long and difficult, but I was no longer alone. Steve Mills had given me a gift that day—the gift of being heard, of being seen. I wasn't just an inmate with a number; I was a person with a story that deserved to be told.

From that day on, everything changed. I felt a fire inside me, a determination to prove my innocence, not just for myself but for everyone who had been wronged by a system that didn't care about the truth. Steve's belief in me lifted my spirits to a height I can't even put into words. I felt empowered, motivated, and ready to face whatever challenges lay ahead.

That article wasn't just a piece of newsprint; it was a beacon of hope, a sign that maybe, just maybe, justice could be served. And with that hope in my heart, I vowed to keep fighting, no matter how long it took. Because now, I knew I wasn't alone. I had Steve Mills by my side, and together, we were going to prove the truth.

Deon's Thoughts

December 19, 2001, marked the day my life started to shift, a day that felt like an early birthday gift from the universe. My birthday was just around the corner on December 21st, and after years of darkness and despair, the first glimmer of hope finally shone through the bars of my cell.

I remember holding that article in my hands, trembling with a mixture of disbelief and cautious optimism. The headline, "New Doubts About Confessions" by Steve Mills, was the first sign that our voices were being heard by someone other than the people who had denied us our constitutional rights for so long. For nine years, we had been fighting an uphill battle, screaming into the void, hoping that someone—anyone—would listen and believe in our innocence.

When I first saw my name in print, alongside those of my co-defendants, it was like a lifeline had been thrown to us in the middle of a stormy sea. Steve Mills, along with Marie Posley and Ken Armstrong, became more than just journalists—they became our lifeboats. They entered our lives at a time when we were drowning in a sea of hopelessness, and their words began to chip away at the walls that had confined us.

As I read through the article, I felt a surge of emotions that I hadn't allowed myself to feel in years. Hope was a dangerous thing in a place like this, where it could be snatched away just as quickly as it came. But this... this was different. The words on the page were a beacon, lighting the way to what we all desperately wanted—the truth.

The article brought our story to the world in a way that nothing else had. It wasn't just another piece of paper; it was our voice, our truth, finally being broadcasted to the masses. Within days, our story was everywhere. We were on Fox News, CNN, and every major news outlet you could think of. People were finally starting to listen to us, to see that we were truly innocent men, wrongly imprisoned for a crime we didn't commit.

For the first time in nearly a decade, I felt like this nightmare might actually be coming to an end. The article wasn't just a glimmer of hope; it was a floodlight that pierced through the darkness that had surrounded us for so long. It gave us something to hold onto, something to believe in as we continued to fight for our freedom.

The days that followed were a blur of interviews, news segments, and conversations with our legal team. We were no longer just inmates; we were men with a story that the world wanted to hear. And that story was starting to make a difference.

But with hope came fear. Fear that it would all be taken away, that this newfound attention would fizzle out and leave us in the same place we had been for years. The article was a beginning, but it was also a reminder that the fight wasn't over. We had a long road ahead of us, but for the first time in a long time, we could see the end of it.

December 19, 2001, will forever be etched in my memory as the day our voices started to matter. It was the beginning of the end of our nightmare, a chapter in our story that would eventually lead to our freedom. And as I sat in my cell, reading those words over and over, I couldn't help but think that maybe, just maybe, this was the start of something bigger than any of us could have imagined.

Chapter 12

When The Truth Is All You Have

Daniel's Thoughts

When the first article about my case was published, titled "Cops and Confessions," I was filled with an overwhelming sense of hope. For the first time in years, it felt like someone was listening, that the world outside was finally starting to see the tragedy of what had happened to me. Meeting Steve Mills, the journalist who wrote the piece, was a moment of validation. I had spent hours with him, going over every detail of my case, meticulously showing him the evidence of my innocence. I poured my heart out, and he seemed to understand the injustice I had suffered.

When that article came out, it was like a beacon in the darkness. It was a public acknowledgment that I wasn't just another inmate, but a man who had been wrongfully convicted. It gave me a glimpse of what I had been longing for all these years: justice. I remember thinking that maybe, just maybe, this would be the turning point. The anticipation of what could happen next consumed me. I started to believe that a motion might be filed soon, one that could finally set me free.

But then, everything came crashing down. A second article was released shortly after the first, titled "When Jail is No Alibi in Murders."

CHICAGO TRIBUNE: *When jail is no alibi in murders; New evidence undercuts state case*

December 19, 2001

By Steve Mills, Maurice Possley and Ken Armstrong

Early on a December morning in 1992, a 17-year-old gang member named Daniel Taylor sat in a windowless police interrogation room and confessed to a double murder committed two weeks earlier in the Uptown neighborhood.

With a detective, a prosecutor and a stenographer in the room, Taylor said he and seven other gang members met at Clarendon Park to plot the murders.

The eight of them, Taylor said, then walked a few blocks to a second-floor apartment on Agatite Avenue. Four waited on the street, acting as lookouts, while Taylor and three others went up to the apartment.

They broke down the door and demanded money from one of the tenants. When he refused, a gang member "shot the guy on the left side of his head, around the temple area," Taylor said in his confession. Then they turned their attention to a woman who lived in the apartment, grabbing her arms.

"Please don't, please don't," she pleaded, according to Taylor's confession.

Twenty-nine minutes after Taylor had begun, prosecutors had the evidence they would need to send him to prison for the rest of his life.

But the case built upon Taylor's confession, like others examined in a Tribune investigation, was not as airtight as it seemed.

Just as he was going to be formally charged with two counts of murder, Taylor protested to detectives that he could not have committed the crimes because he had been in police custody when they occurred.

Within days, police found an arrest report that showed Taylor was locked up for disorderly conduct at 6:45 p.m. on Nov. 16, the night of the murders. A copy of a bond slip showed he had not been released from the Town Hall District lockup until 10 p.m.

The murders occurred at 8:43 p.m., according to police.

But instead of releasing Taylor and questioning how he came to confess, detectives gathered evidence putting Taylor on the street when the murders occurred and casting doubt on his arrest records.

They found a witness--a drug dealer and rival gang member--who said he saw Taylor in Clarendon Park at 7:30 p.m. They found two police officers, Michael Berti and Sean Glinski, who then filed a report saying they emerged from an apartment a half-block from the murders after making a drug arrest and saw Taylor at 9:30 p.m.

The fact that a jury chose to believe Taylor's confession over the police records that documented his arrest and his time in the lockup illustrates the remarkable potency of confessions in the criminal justice system. Taylor's conviction also shows just how difficult it can be for a defendant to disavow his confession, even when he has an alibi supported not by relatives or friends, but by police records.

A Tribune investigation of Taylor's case has uncovered new evidence that supports Taylor's version of events and his contention that his confession was false.

The witness who put Taylor in the park now says he lied at the request of detectives, and later was rewarded with leni-ency on a narcotics charge.

Key portions of the chronology laid out by Berti and Glinski are undermined by recent interviews and records obtained by the Tribune.

And, the Tribune found that four months before Berti and Glinski wrote their report, a Cook County Circuit judge or-dered Berti off the witness stand in an unrelated case and branded him a "liar."

"I didn't do this and they know it," Taylor, now 26, said in one of several interviews at Stateville Correctional Center in Joliet. "I was in jail when this happened. No way I could have committed those murders."

Police and prosecutors involved in Taylor's case declined to comment.

Two other Chicago men have presented the same alibi to refute murder confessions. Peter Williams confessed to murder in 1992--the same year as Taylor--but the charges against him were dropped when police verified that Williams was in jail when the crime occurred. Mario Hayes confessed in 1996, but he was acquitted three years later after producing records that showed he, too, had a jail alibi.

In the murder case that sent Taylor to prison, Chicago police charged eight people in all. Taylor and four others were convicted but the cases against the other three defendants fell apart. One was acquitted at trial and prosecutors dropped charges against the other two after their confessions were thrown out.

But Taylor's alibi raises troubling questions about all of the cases. That is because all the defendants confessed and each said Taylor was with them.

Agatite Avenue murders

Nine hundred and forty people were murdered in Chicago in 1992--more than any year since. Jeffrey Lassiter and Sharon Haugabook were only two of them. Their deaths, in a small second-floor apartment in a brick courtyard build-ing, did not merit a mention in the daily newspapers.

The apartment, at 910 W. Agatite Ave., was rented by Lassiter, a crack-cocaine abuser with a string of arrests. Hauga-book, another drug abuser who also had been arrested numerous times, including for prostitution, had recently moved in.

According to police reports and interviews, Lassiter had long allowed prostitutes from the neighborhood to bring cus-tomers to the apartment if the prostitutes paid him with cocaine.

Several weeks before the murders, Lassiter also allowed a West Side gang member named Dennis Mixon to use the apartment to sell cocaine, according to police reports and Mixon.

On Nov. 16, at 8:43 p.m., neighbors heard gunshots and called police. When detectives arrived, they found the front door broken in and Lassiter and Haugabook on the floor, both of them shot in the head at close range.

Lassiter, 41, was pronounced dead at the scene. Haugabook, 37, was taken to Illinois Masonic Hospital, where she died without regaining consciousness.

Police found no eyewitnesses to the shooting, but another building resident, Faye McCoy, told detectives that she looked out her window after she heard the shots and saw four men walking out. One of them, she said, pointed a finger at her in warning.

One of the first people detectives sought was Mixon, after a confidential informant told them that Mixon was involved in the murders, according to police reports.

Detectives showed Mixon's mug shot to McCoy, who identified him as one of the four men leaving the building that night. Mixon, police

When The Truth Is All You Have

learned, also had been in "an altercation" with Lassiter a few weeks earlier over a VCR. Police were unable to locate him.

The murders were still unsolved two weeks later when, on Dec. 2, patrol officers spotted Lewis Gardner, 15, and Akia Phillips, 19, trying to sell drugs on a street corner and took them into custody.

During questioning, officers said Gardner, whose IQ of 70 indicated borderline mental retardation, told them that he got his drugs from Deon Patrick and that Patrick was involved in the murders.

According to detectives who took over the questioning, Gardner quickly admitted a role in the murders--that of a look-out. Phillips, police said, also volunteered to help the detectives solve the murders and then, like Gardner, confessed he was a lookout.

Gardner and Phillips, according to police, implicated the rest of the defendants--Taylor, Mixon, Joseph Brown, Phillips' brother Paul, Rodney Mathews and Patrick.

A few hours later, just after 2 a.m., four detectives arrived at the youth home where he was staying, and roused a sleep-ing Taylor. The detectives allowed him to dress, and then took him away for questioning.

Lifetime of trauma

One way or another, Daniel Taylor has been in the custody of the state of Illinois for most of his life.

He became a ward of the Department of Children and Family Services in February 1986, at age 11, though the state first took him away from his mother three years earlier because of her cocaine use.

Taylor was one of four children; he never knew his father. His mother, Debra, now 44 and working as a hospital records analyst, said that Daniel struggled with behavioral problems, particularly a temper.

DCFS has discarded most of Taylor's records, a routine practice when wards "age out" of the system. But what few records remain reveal a youth shunted from one foster home or shelter to another. By his own count, Taylor lived in more than a dozen different homes or facilities grow-ing up.

The remaining records make note of a wide variety of incidents, large and small. One time he threw pepper at a girl. Another time he ran away and stole a car.

Taylor recalls those years as a time when he was increasingly angry and resentful at how his mother's drug use had shat-tered the family.

"Being in the state, having no family that's your blood, it gets to you sometimes," he said. "It's almost like jail. It's not really home."

He turned to the Vice Lords about three months before he was arrested for the murder. His friends were Vice Lords, he said, so it made sense to him to join them.

They sold drugs, mostly small amounts of cocaine and marijuana, and liked to hang around Clarendon Park, he said.

Before the Lassiter and Haugabook murders, Taylor had been arrested five times, all in the four months before the slay-ings--three times for mob action and twice for theft, police records show.

Many versions of same story

Three hours after Taylor arrived at the now-closed Area 6 detective headquarters, he gave a 27-page court-reported con-fession.

Detective Brian Killacky would later testify that Taylor first denied that he knew anything about the murders. Killacky said he then read Taylor his rights and, without any prompting, Taylor "almost immediately" admitted taking part in the murders.

Taylor's account is dramatically different.

Killacky and Detective Anthony Villardita entered the room and, said Taylor, asked what he knew of the murders. Tay-lor, who was handcuffed to a chair, denied knowing anything, he said. The detectives told him Gardner and Phillips had already implicated him.

When Taylor persisted in his denials, the detectives hit him once in the side with a flashlight, he said, yelled at him and told him they would let him go if he confessed.

Finally, Taylor said, he decided to tell the detectives what they wanted to hear. He said he believed that resisting further was futile, and that the detectives would make good on their promise to release him.

"They said, 'We don't want you. You're not the one. We really want Rodney Mathews and Deon Patrick,' " Taylor said in an interview.

Taylor said his confession was made up of details he picked up from the detectives' questions, from information he had heard on the street and from Akia Phillips' confession, which they gave him to read.

"I just sort of put it all together," Taylor said.

In the confession, Taylor said that he, Mathews, Patrick and Mixon went to Lassiter's apartment to collect a $200 or $300 drug debt owed to Mixon. Gardner, brothers Akia and Paul Phillips, and Brown stayed outside as lookouts.

When Lassiter said he did not have the money, according to the confession, Patrick shot him. Patrick then shot Hauga-book as Taylor and Mixon held her arms.

On the last page of Taylor's confession, Assistant State's Atty. Joe Magats noted the time: 5:52 a.m.

Taylor was then put in a line-up where Faye McCoy, the woman who lived in the building and saw a group of men leav-ing after the shooting, was asked if she recognized him.

McCoy said she had seen Taylor in the neighborhood before, but she was certain he was not one of the four men she saw after the murders.

In an interview with the Tribune, McCoy said detectives pressed her to implicate Taylor, sometimes coming to her home in the middle of the night to get her to say she saw Taylor at the building. But she refused.

"They told me, 'They say they did it,' " said McCoy, 51, a neighborhood activist who has served on local school coun-cils. "They kept on bringing me pictures and trying to get me to say it was them."

After the line-up, Taylor was jolted when he was told he was being held on murder charges. He said he searched his mind for where he was Nov. 16.

He remembered a court date, Nov. 19, and worked backward to recall that he had been arrested the night Lassiter and Haugabook were slain and could not have been involved. He then blurted out that he had been in the lockup.

Even after detectives found records that showed Taylor had indeed been arrested and locked up, Taylor still did not go free.

Three months later, detectives arrested Mixon and said that he confessed as well. Mixon told police that when the eight defendants met at Clarendon Park before they went to Lassiter's apartment, Taylor said he had just been released from the police lockup.

Mixon's confession is the only one that was made after police learned of the lockup records that gave Taylor an alibi. It also is the only confession to work Taylor's time in police custody into the narrative of the murders, providing details that would bolster the police account of what happened that night.

Taylor's case goes to trial

By the time Taylor came to trial in late August 1995, three of his co-defendants had been set free. In one case, Judge Thomas Hett ruled that the arrest was illegal--and the confession should be thrown out--because there was insufficient evidence to take him into custody. In another, he ruled that a detective's promise to drop unrelated drug charges was an improper inducement to confess.

In the third, a jury acquitted Rodney Mathews, who said that he confessed only because detectives mistreated him.

"When they chain you up to the wall, that's something," Mathews said in an interview. "No food. Nothing. I pissed my-self. Then you get all tired.

"That's how you sign it. Your heart, man, everything is gone. I was just really tired. I was wet. I just couldn't take it no more."

For Taylor's jury, the issue was simple: Was he in the apartment on Agatite Avenue when Lassiter and Haugabook were shot, or was he in custody in the Town Hall District lockup at Addison and Halsted Streets?

The prosecution was led by Thomas Needham, the son of a high-ranking Chicago police officer and later a top aide to Mayor Richard M. Daley. Currently, he works as the chief of staff at the city Police Department and is on the governor's commission studying reform of the death penalty in Illinois.

When Needham and prosecutor Jeanne Bischoff entered Hett's courtroom for Taylor's trial, their best piece of evidence against Taylor was his confession.

Fingerprints found in Lassiter's apartment did not match Taylor or his co-defendants; no DNA was found that linked Taylor or the other defendants to the murders; and police never recovered the murder weapon.

To challenge Taylor's arrest and lockup records, the prosecutors called Adrian Grimes, a convicted drug dealer who testified that he saw Taylor at Clarendon Park at about 7:30 p.m. That put Taylor at the park 45 minutes after his arrest and more than an hour before the 8:43 p.m. murders.

Prosecutors also offered testimony from Officer Sean Glinski, who with

Officer Michael Berti filed the Dec. 14 report that they saw Taylor on the street--and not in jail--around 9:30 p.m.

Glinski said he was one of several officers who responded to a radio bulletin of the shooting. When one of the officers tried to question a youth spotted in an alley less than a half-block from the murder scene, the youth fled into a second-floor apartment and Glinski and other officers followed.

The apartment was the home of Akia and Paul Phillips and their mother Andrea. Officers said that they found a small amount of cocaine there and arrested the mother.

Glinski testified that when the officers left the apartment, he encountered Taylor and asked Taylor to help him find one of Phillips' sons. Glinski said that he, Berti and Taylor drove around for 10 or 15 minutes looking for the boy. Police then dropped off Taylor at 10 p.m. at the Columbus-Maryville shelter, on Montrose Avenue.

Taylor's attorney, Nathan Diamond-Falk, forced Glinski to admit that his report was filed almost two weeks after Taylor asserted his alibi and a month after the encounter.

Glinski also acknowledged that the report was not approved by a supervisor, as department rules require, and that the report of the drug arrest never mentioned the encounter with Taylor.

Like the prosecution, the defense relied on the testimony and the records of police officers.

Officer Terrence Duffy testified that he arrested Taylor across the street from Clarendon Park at 6:45 p.m. on the night of the murders. Taylor, he said, had been screaming and jumping around. He was charged with disorderly conduct.

Duffy drove Taylor to the Town Hall District police station, and handcuffed Taylor to a metal ring on the wall. He moved him to the lockup at 7:25 p.m.--about the same time the prosecution put Taylor in the park.

Lockup keeper John Meindl testified that he left for the evening at 9:15 p.m. or 9:30 p.m. and that Taylor was still in the lockup.

Officer James Gillespie testified he started work at the station's front desk at 9:30 p.m. and issued Taylor's bond slip, which said 10 p.m., although he could not recall if he saw Taylor when he was released.

Diamond-Falk also called a handwriting expert, who said that the signature on the bond slip appeared to be Taylor's.

Taylor did not testify.

In closing arguments, Needham and Bischoff sought to discredit the officers who had testified for Taylor, accusing them of covering up sloppy record keeping for fear they would be blamed for letting Taylor leave jail early to commit the murders.

"Paperwork is not foolproof," Bischoff said. "But I'll tell you what is foolproof. And what is foolproof are the defen-dant's own words."

Diamond-Falk, in his closing, argued that the arrest report and bond slip showed definitively that Taylor was in custody when the murders occurred.

"There isn't one reasonable doubt in this case. The whole case is doubtful," he said. "The whole case is one big doubt despite the statement."

Jurors began deliberating late in the afternoon on September 7. By that evening, they had reached their verdict: guilty.

"A couple people were skeptical for maybe a couple minutes, but once we figured it out, it was pretty easy," one juror, Donald Borta, said in an interview.

Borta said jurors found it easy to believe that the records from the lockup officers were wrong. They could not imagine a false confession.

"The only piece that didn't seem to fit was that stuff that he'd been in jail at the time," said Daniel Cacchione, another former juror. "He could have walked out the back door for all we knew. Who knew if he was really in jail?"

Taylor was sentenced to life in prison.

Mixon, who was tried simultaneously by a separate jury, was convicted as well and also sentenced to life.

In an interview at Stateville Correctional Center, Mixon acknowledged he was in the building courtyard around the time of the murders. But he denied that he was involved. He insisted that Taylor and the six other defendants were wrongly charged.

"The guys they had in this case with me, they never set foot in that apartment," Mixon said. "Daniel Taylor, he wasn't even there."

New documents cast doubts

The testimony at Taylor's trial told only part of the story.

Adrian Grimes, a prosecution witness, told the Tribune that he lied when he testified before a grand jury and at trial that Taylor was at the park a short time before the murders occurred.

He said that while the trial was under way, he was picked up on a felony narcotics charge that had been dismissed for a lack of evidence earlier that year. But prosecutors re-indicted him and an arrest warrant was issued that allowed police to take him into custody.

Grimes said two police officers, whose names he could not recall, threatened to keep him locked up if he did not coop-erate in the Taylor case.

"I wasn't even at the park," Grimes said in an interview in Logan Correctional Center in Lincoln, where he is serving time for drug possession. "But [the police] kept saying, 'If you testify this guy right here was at the park, we'll let you go.'

"They told me, 'Won't nobody care about him. He ain't got no family. It won't be nobody's loss.'"

Two months after he testified at Taylor's trial, Grimes pleaded guilty. Although he faced one to three years in prison, he was given two years conditional discharge and was not even required to report to a probation officer.

"Mr. Grimes was a material witness to a homicide which resulted in a conviction," a prosecutor told the judge. "This was not part of his plea agreement in regards to his testifying but because he did testify and because there was two con-victions, that's why we're asking for two years conditional discharge on this matter."

Grimes said he now regrets his part in Taylor's trial.

"My intention wasn't to hurt no one. Only thing they wanted me to do is point him out and say he was at the park," Grimes said. "But they used me to destroy a perfectly good young man's life."

McCoy, another prosecution witness, told the Tribune that before she took the witness stand, prosecutors--like police had done--tried to get her to say more. They hurried her to their offices, she said, and showed her Taylor's confession.

"They were giving me little things they wanted me to say," McCoy said. "And I wouldn't cooperate. I wouldn't lie. They said it's not lying because it's in the confessions. They just wanted the boys. And if those boys had been there, I sure would have said so, no problem."

The Tribune also has obtained documents that cast doubt on the testimony by Glinski and the report that he and his partner, Berti, filed.

Their report said that after they arrested Andrea Phillips on the drug charge, they came outside and saw Taylor on the street, around 9:30 p.m. They said they dropped him off at the Columbus-Maryville shelter around 10 p.m.

Shelter records obtained from DCFS, however, show that Taylor did not arrive at Maryville until 3 a.m. the following morning.

What's more, Phillips said in an interview that she recalled that the officers did not leave her apartment until after 10 p.m. because they stayed to watch a TV news report about police officers with criminal records. A report on that subject was, in fact, the lead story broadcast on WMAQ-Ch. 5 news the night of the murders.

Taylor said that after his release from the lockup, he walked to the Phillips' home and arrived around 10:30 p.m. or 10:45 p.m. He said he never encountered Berti and Glinski that night. He remained at the apartment, he said, until early the next morning.

Phillips, who had been arrested that night, said that while she was still at the Town Hall station, she called the apartment and told Taylor to leave. She said she believed the drugs found in the apartment were Taylor's and that he was responsi-ble for her arrest. Police reports obtained by the Tribune say that she made a call about 1:30 a.m.

Taylor recalled that after Phillips called to order him out, he walked to Maryville.

The Tribune also uncovered the transcript of a court hearing from August 1992, four months before Berti and Glinski filed their key report, that raises questions about Berti's credibility.

During a pretrial hearing in an unrelated murder case, then-Cook County Circuit Judge Earl Strayhorn took the extremely rare action of ordering Berti off the witness stand in mid testimony, declaring, "I don't believe a thing he says. He goes down in my book as a liar."

The Tribune also discovered police reports in the files prosecutors turned over to one of Taylor's co-defendants that Taylor's lawyer said he never received.

One report, dated December 29, reads: "Need to locate James Anderson concerning the Lassiter Homicide. Anderson was locked up in

023 District with [Taylor] . . . ." A report two days after that indicates that the police were still looking for Anderson.

At the time, Anderson was a cocaine and marijuana abuser who had a lengthy record of arrests and convictions, mostly for theft. He took many of his meals at a Salvation Army shelter.

In an interview with the Tribune at the Champaign County Jail, where he was being held on a bad-check charge, Ander-son said that the police did find him. He recalled that he had been arrested on the day of the murders on a warrant for retail theft.

He could not recall the names of the detectives who interviewed him, but he said that he told them that he remembered being in a cell that evening with a young black man.

"I told them I remembered being in with a kid," Anderson said in the interview. "I said I remembered the kid. But then they sort of lost interest."

Under the law, prosecutors are required to turn over evidence that could be favorable to the defense. Diamond-Falk said he doesn't remember prosecutors giving him those reports and could not find them in his files. Prosecutors Needham and Bischoff declined to comment.

Diamond-Falk said the reports could have been used to find Anderson and bolster Taylor's alibi. "Why didn't I get this? Why?" he asked, looking at the papers. "I should have gotten this."

Diamond-Falk said that he did not hire an investigator to work on the case with him; instead, he tried to do his own pre-trial investigation.

His itemized bill to the court, charging $7,028 to defend Taylor, shows that Diamond-Falk did about 15 hours of case investigation. That included four hours meeting with Taylor at the jail, and two hours timing various drives, such as from the youth home where Taylor had been staying to the Area 6 violent crimes unit office at Belmont and Western Avenues where he was interrogated.

Diamond-Falk conceded that he should have retrieved the Maryville records because they were critical to bolstering Taylor's alibi. He said he never tried to track down any of the prisoners who might have been in the lockup with Taylor.

"I'm a . . . moron," he said, shaking his head.

Out of touch with the world

Since coming to Stateville prison, Taylor has received his GED, and he works as a teacher's aide, making $45 a month. He has little contact with the outside world. Most of his friends do not accept his collect calls, the only kind that can be made from prison.

He also has lost touch with his family and has had only sporadic phone contact with his mother. She has never come to see him. Now, he can hardly remember her face.

"All I can remember, really, is that she's dark-skinned like me," he said.

His first appeal was denied in 1998 by a three-judge panel of the Illinois Appellate Court.

Earlier this year, he filed a second appeal on his own, using the prison's law library to research legal issues and consult-ing other inmates. Judge Bertina Lampkin dismissed that petition.

Taylor said that he was not surprised by Lampkin's ruling but still was disappointed.

"I don't understand how I can be in here," he said. "How many times can somebody say they can prove their innocence like me?"

New evidence undermines Daniel Taylor's conviction

Early in the morning on Dec. 3, 1992, after Chicago Police detectives roused him from sleep at a youth shelter, 17-year-old Daniel Taylor confessed to the murder of two people in an Uptown apartment. But records showed that Taylor was being held at a police station on an unrelated charge the night of the killings. A jury convicted Taylor despite his alibi, and he was sentenced to life in prison. A Tribune investigation found evidence bolstering Taylor's claim of innocence.

The night of the crime: Conflicting accounts of Nov. 16, 1992

8:43 p.m. Time of murders

Site of murders: 910 W. Agatite Ave.

1. Town Hall District police station

2. Phillips' apartment

3. Youth shelter

PROSECUTION'S EVIDENCE

7 p.m. In his confession, Taylor said he was meeting with fellow gang members in Clarendon Park.

7:30 p.m. Convicted drug dealer Adrian Grimes testifies that he saw

Taylor at Clarendon Park. Grimes later told the Tribune he wasn't even at the park.

9:30 p.m. Officer Sean Glinski testifies he and Officer Michael Berti saw Taylor on the street after arresting Andrea Phillips in her apartment (2 on map). He said Taylor rode in a police car with him for 10 or 15 minutes helping him look for Phillips' son.

10 p.m. Glinski testifies he and Berti dropped off Taylor at the Columbus-Maryville youth shelter (3 on map) on Mon-trose Avenue.

Nearly a month after the murders--after police learned Taylor had an alibi--Berti and Glinski filed a report (above) say-ing they had seen Taylor on Nov. 16. It was not signed by a supervisor.

TAYLOR'S CO-DEFENDANTS

Seven other people confessed to taking part in the crime.

- Four defendants also were convicted, with sentences ranging from 30 years in prison to a life sentence.

- Three defendants were freed. A judge ruled that police had illegally arrested one and improperly promised to drop unrelated charges against another. A jury acquitted the third.

EVIDENCE USED IN TAYLOR'S DEFENSE

6:45 p.m. Taylor was arrested near Clarendon Park for disorderly conduct, a police report shows. He was taken to Town Hall District station (1 on map) at Addison and Halsted Streets.

7:25 p.m. Records show Taylor was moved into the lockup at the station.

Between 9:15-9:30 p.m. Taylor still was in the lockup, an officer who left the station at that time testified.

10 p.m. Taylor was released from the lockup, a bond slip (right) shows.

DISCOVERED DURING TRIBUNE INVESTIGATION

Shortly after 10 p.m. Andrea Phillips said Berti and Glinski did not leave her apartment until after they had watched the first part of a 10 p.m. newscast about police misconduct.

Between 10:30 and 10:45 p.m. Taylor, a friend of Phillips' son, says he walked to the apartment after he was released from the lockup.

1:30 a.m. Police reports show Phillips placed a phone call from the station. She says she called home and told Taylor to leave when she found out he was there.

3 a.m. Computer records show Taylor arrived at the Columbus-Maryville youth shelter on Montrose.

Sources: Court and Chicago Police Department records, Illinois Department of Children and Family Services, Tribune interviews

Daniel's Feedback

This article challenged everything. Reading it felt like a punch to the gut. I went from feeling on top of the world to feeling completely defeated. It's hard to explain just how crushing that moment was. Physically, I felt like I'd been hit by a truck. Mentally and emotionally, I was drained, as if every ounce of hope that had filled me up was violently sucked out, leaving a void I didn't know how to fill.

I didn't want to exist anymore. The new article had highlighted supposed flaws in my alibi, casting doubt on what had seemed so clear just days before. And then, to make matters worse, my appeal was put together and subsequently denied. Just like that, every hope I had built up, every piece of newfound energy that had surged through me, was gone. I was empty. I felt like I was drowning in despair, suffocated by the weight of this injustice.

Yet, somehow, in the depths of this despair, I found something to hold on to. I knew I was innocent. I knew my co-defendants were innocent. That knowledge, that undeniable truth, became the thing I clung to. It was the only thing that kept me going. I couldn't give up, not on myself and not on them. We hadn't done this. We didn't deserve this.

I thought about the old saying my parents and elders had always repeated: "If you tell the truth, the truth will always reveal itself." Growing up, I believed that with all my heart. I was born in 1975, and my parents drilled it into me that the truth is powerful, that it can cut through any lie, any deception. "The truth will set you free," they said. But they never told me how long it would take. They never told me that sometimes, the truth takes its sweet time revealing itself, testing every ounce of patience and resolve you have.

In those dark moments, when I felt like giving up, I remembered those words. I held on to them with everything I had. I told myself that even though I was deep in this pit of despair, I had to press on. I couldn't let myself be consumed by the darkness. I had to keep fighting, keep pushing, because the truth was all I had.

Slowly, I pulled myself out of that dark place. I let go of the self-pity, the loathing, the desire to just give up, and found a way to push through. I realized that I couldn't afford to let this break me. I had to stay strong, not just for myself, but for my co-defendants, for everyone who believed in my innocence.

But when I say the denial of my appeal was devastating, I mean it. I've never experienced pain like that. The only thing I can compare it to is the loss of a family member, a mother, or a father. It's that kind of soul-crushing hurt that leaves you feeling like you're barely holding on. But even that doesn't fully capture the magnitude of what I felt.

Despite everything, I knew I had to continue. I had to keep going, keep fighting, keep believing that one day, the truth would come to light. That's all I had left, and I wasn't about to let it go.

Chapter 13

A Ray of Light in the Darkness

Daniel's Thoughts

I remember the day vividly—January 2, 2003. I was in my cell, trying to muster the strength to keep fighting, to keep believing that one day the truth would prevail. It wasn't easy. Every day felt like a relentless battle, a constant push and pull between hope and despair. I'd been pushing for so long, trying to prove my innocence, trying to find the energy to press on despite the constant rejections and the unyielding walls of the justice system.

Steve Mills, the news reporter, had been a beacon of light in these dark times. We worked together tirelessly, combing through every detail of the case, re-examining every piece of evidence, every statement, every angle. We wanted to make sure that the story we were putting out to the public was accurate and thorough. It was our way of fighting back, of keeping the truth alive. Steve knew my story, and he believed in my innocence. That belief was like a lifeline for me.

When the article, "New Doubts Cast on Verdict; Inmate Disputes Guilt of 4 Others Convicted of '92 Double Murder," came out, I felt a surge of confidence. It wasn't just about the words printed on the page; it was about being heard. It was about someone, anyone, taking notice of the injustice that had been done to me. There was a renewed sense of hope—a belief that maybe, just maybe, the truth was finally breaking through the cracks of this broken system.

CHICAGO TRIBUNE: New doubts cast on verdict; Inmate disputes guilt of 4 others convicted of '92 double murder

January 2, 2003

In 1993, Daniel Taylor was convicted of a double murder and sentenced to life in prison, even though his alibi--that he was in jail when the murders were committed--was supported by an arrest report and a bond slip.

Now, interviews with one of Taylor's co-defendants and a potential witness further bolster Taylor's claim of innocence, and suggest that three other men who also were convicted may be innocent as well.

Last month, Dennis Mixon gave the Tribune a detailed account of the murders that included his admission that he was involved and the name of a man that Mixon says fired the fatal shots.

Taylor and Mixon were among eight young men who Chicago police said all confessed to the Nov. 16, 1992, murders of Jeffrey Lassiter, 41, and Sharon Haugabook, 37, inside a North Side apartment.

The questionable evidence against Taylor was first detailed in December 2001, in a story published as part of the Trib-une series "Cops and Confessions," which examined how illegal and improper police tactics can lead to false and coerced confessions. Taylor and his co-defendants have disavowed their confessions, saying the police tricked them or coerced them to confess.

Prompted by the article, Cook County State's Atty. Richard Devine reviewed the case and launched a grand jury inves-tigation. Marcy Jensen, a spokeswoman for Devine, said recently that the inquiry pursued a number of leads and that they all "have come up empty." The office's investigation, according to Jensen, is continuing.

Besides Taylor and Mixon, three others remain in prison--Lewis Gardner, Deon Patrick and Paul Phillips. Taylor, Mixon and Patrick are serving life sentences at Stateville Correctional Center. Gardner and Phillips are serving 30-year sentences at Danville Correctional Center.

In the interview, Mixon said that Taylor, Gardner, Patrick and Phillips were not connected in any way with the crime.

The Hazel Boyz

"I had never seen those guys before," Mixon, now 41, said of his co-defendants, most of whom were a decade younger. "I met them in jail."

Mixon said the confrontation that led to the double murder was not over a drug debt, as police and prosecutors alleged, but over $300 worth of missing electronics equipment.

His account is supported by two other people interviewed by the Tribune--a man who says he was outside the building where the murders occurred and Mixon's former girlfriend.

The man, Willie Lee Triplett, who was not interviewed by police during their investigation, said he saw Mixon leave the building just as the gunshots were fired. But Triplett, who described himself as a recovering drug addict, said that among the men convicted in the case, only Mixon was there.

"I know for 100 percent, these ain't the guys that did it," said Triplett, after viewing photographs of Taylor and his other co-defendants in an interview in Madison, Wis., where he lives and works.

"They didn't do no murder. I know that for a fact. I was there ... I will go to court and tell the judge it ain't these people. I will do that."

Ex-girlfriend's corroboration

Mixon's former girlfriend and the mother of three of his children, also corroborated portions of Mixon's account. Joezana Tyler said that Mixon told her years ago, as well as more recently, that Taylor and the others had no part in the murders.

She said in an interview in her South Side apartment that in a conversation after the murders, Mixon "told me he was there."

"He said he couldn't believe how everything was happening so fast, so fast," she recalled. "I told him, 'You need to tell the truth.' He got quiet. I told him that those two [murder victims] were calling from the grave to hear the truth."

The case began when police were called to the third-floor apartment at 910 W. Agatite Ave. shortly after 8:43 p.m., after several gunshots were heard. They found Lassiter dead on the floor and Haugabook seriously wounded. She died later at a hospital without regaining consciousness.

According to Chicago police and Cook County prosecutors, Taylor, Mixon and six other defendants met at Clarendon Park earlier that evening and decided to go to Lassiter's apartment and recover drug money that Lassiter allegedly owed to Mixon.

Four of them, including Taylor and Mixon, went into the apartment, while the other four served as lookouts, police and prosecutors alleged.

Within days after the murders, police and prosecutors obtained confessions from seven of the defendants but still were searching for Mixon, who was not arrested for several months.

But there was a problem. In each confession, the suspects said that Taylor was with them, even though the police later discovered police records that showed Taylor was in a lockup at the Town Hall District, at Halsted and Addison Streets.

Arrested for disturbance

Taylor, according to those police reports, was arrested at 6:45 p.m., for causing a disturbance on the street. He was held until 10 p.m., when a Police Department bond slip shows that he was released. The murders, according to police, oc-curred at 8:43 p.m.

Taylor told detectives of his arrest, but not until after he confessed. Then 17, he said he knew he was innocent but only belatedly recalled where he had been the night of the murders. At the time, Taylor lived on the streets and in various youth shelters.

Detectives checked out Taylor's claim and found records of his arrest and his time in the jail lockup, throwing their case into jeopardy and threatening to undermine the cases against the six other co-defendants.

Police then gathered evidence undercutting Taylor's alibi, arguing that the arrest and lockup records could not be trusted. Weeks after the murders, two officers provided a report saying they saw Taylor on the street around 8:45 p.m. while they were making an unrelated drug arrest a block away from the crime.

The report was crucial because it put Taylor close to the crime scene at a key time.

The officers said in their report that they picked up Taylor and drove around with him looking for another young man, then dropped off Taylor at DCFS' Columbus Maryville facility on Montrose Avenue.

Police also located a small-time drug dealer named Adrian Grimes. At Taylor's trial, Grimes testified that he saw Taylor in Clarendon Park at the alleged planning meeting after 6:45 p.m.

The Hazel Boyz

Nearly four months after Taylor and the others were charged, Mixon was arrested. He confessed and implicated Taylor and the others. But Mixon's confession contained a new element--that when Taylor arrived at Clarendon Park for the meeting, he told the other men he had just been released from the lockup.

Police and prosecutors had enough to persuade a jury to convict Taylor and four of the original eight defendants. Three others arrested in the case went free--two of them because charges against them were thrown out because of problems with their arrest and the way detectives interrogated them, and one because he was found not guilty at trial.

The Tribune's re-investigation of the case in 2001 turned up new evidence that revealed problems with the evidence against Taylor.

Leniency traded for testimony

Grimes, in an interview in prison, said that he had lied about Taylor and court records showed that he was rewarded with leniency in an unrelated narcotics case. Grimes said he gave the testimony at the request of police detectives.

The Tribune also located documents supporting Taylor's version of events from that night. Though police maintained he was returned to the Maryville facility at 10 p.m., records from the state Department of Children and Family Services show Taylor arriving at 3 a.m.

In an initial interview with the Tribune in 2001, Mixon denied any involvement in the murders but did acknowledge that he was in the building's courtyard at the time. Although he maintained that none of the other defendants were involved, he would not elaborate.

His most current account puts him squarely in the center of events leading up to the murder, though he still maintains he was not in the apartment when the shooting began.

The apartment was rented by Lassiter, a crack-cocaine user, and often frequented by Haugabook, a drug abuser with a history of prostitution arrests. Mixon said he stayed there at times as well and kept some of his belongings there.

On the day of the murders, Mixon said, he had gone to the apartment to get some the electronic equipment. Mixon said Lassiter told him the items were gone but that Mixon could recover them somewhere on the West Side, and he gave Mixon an address.

A Ray of Light in the Darkness

Mixon, a Vice Lord, said he called a fellow street gang member and drug dealer and asked him for a ride to the address. The man, whose name Mixon gave to the Tribune, picked him up. Also with the other Vice Lord were two other men whose names Mixon says he does not recall.

When the address supplied by Lassiter turned out to be vacant, the four men returned to Lassiter's, Mixon said. One man stayed in the car, while Mixon, the man Mixon identified as the killer and a third man walked up the stairs to the apart-ment.

Mixon said that he fled the apartment when one of the men threatened to shoot and wound Lassiter and Haugabook. Mixon said that he rushed downstairs and heard the shots as he emerged from the building. At the same time, he said he saw Triplett, a man he knew from Crane Tech High School and also from selling drugs.

After the two other men came downstairs, Mixon said, the one he knew admitted that he had just killed Lassiter and Haugabook.

That man is now awaiting trial for an unrelated murder. His attorney acknowledged that the man had received a letter from the Tribune outlining Mixon's accusation. The lawyer said he instructed the man not to discuss the case and declined further comment.

Mixon said that after the shooting, he and the others--but not Triplett--left in a car.

Triplett, who talked to the Tribune before Mixon gave his most recent account, told a similar story in his interview. He said he was in the doorway when Mixon came downstairs and told him to leave. Then, Triplett said, two other men came out of the building. One of them put a gun in his face and said, "You didn't see nothing."

He found bodies, not drugs

Triplett said he walked out of the courtyard, but a moment later turned back, went upstairs and peeked into the apart-ment. He said he was hoping to find drugs, but he saw Lassiter and Haugabook lying on the floor and on or near a couch, as police said they discovered them.

Triplett said that before the murders he frequently bought crack cocaine from Mixon, and sometimes he got high in the apartment where Lassiter and Haugabook were killed and in the courtyard. In the interview, Triplett said he never saw Mixon after that night.

In the months after the shooting, Mixon said he began to use increasing amounts of cocaine and heroin. Tyler, the girl-friend, said he also had nightmares about what had happened.

"He was different after that. It was like he seen a ghost," Tyler said. "He woke up crying and hollering." She eventually turned him in to police.

Mixon said that when he was arrested, he was carrying some drugs, which he swallowed to avoid detection. The drugs, he said, made him sick and vulnerable to detectives pressuring him to confess and to implicate the seven other suspects.

He said that police told him that they would help him if he told them what they wanted to hear. He said he believed them because his father was a Chicago police officer and he thought the other officers might even let him go as a professional courtesy.

"We struggled back and forth and I finally said, 'OK. Let's go. I'll give you what you want,'" Mixon said.

Statement rehearsed

He said detectives, and later a prosecutor, rehearsed the statement with him, and that he then repeated it to a court reporter who transcribed it. Detective Thomas Johnson, who took Mixon's confession, could not be reached, but detec-tives in the investigation have repeatedly denied any wrongdoing.

"I thought they were going to let me go. I really did," Mixon said. "I was really messed up."

Mixon was put in a lineup and was identified by a tenant in the building, Faye McCoy, who told police that she looked out of her window after the shots were fired and saw Mixon and three other men walking away.

McCoy told police that Taylor and the other co-defendants--men she recognized from the neighborhood -- were not with Mixon at the time.

Mixon told the Tribune that he is now telling the truth in the hope of having a chance at someday being free, although his account leaves him liable for murder under the state's accountability laws. Mixon said he would cooperate with Cook County prosecutors and give them the name of the man whom he believes committed the murders.

Mixon said he hopes his admissions will lead to justice for the defendants in the case.

"I can sleep better," he said.

A Ray of Light in the Darkness

Daniel's Feedback

Even as I felt that hope, I knew deep down that this was going to be a fight. I had been in this struggle long enough to know that they weren't just going to apologize and release me. They weren't going to admit that they were wrong in charging me, convicting me, and sentencing me to life without parole. No, this was going to be a battle—a long, exhausting battle where every inch gained would be hard-fought.

Not long after the article was published, an attorney came on board and filed some petitions on my behalf. I remember feeling a glimmer of optimism—a small light in the darkness that surrounded me. For once, I had someone in my corner who wasn't just a public defender appointed by the courts. This attorney seemed different, more invested in my case, more determined to fight for me. I dared to hope again.

But that hope was short-lived. The petition was denied due to some procedural error—another technicality, another blow. I got a letter from the attorney explaining the denial and wishing me luck in my quest for freedom. It was like being punched in the gut. All the air left my lungs, and for a moment, I just sat there, staring at the letter, unable to process what I was reading. It felt like the universe was mocking me, dangling freedom in front of me only to snatch it away again.

I had no money to afford a private attorney, and I knew that the road ahead was going to be even tougher. I was at a point where most of the legal work had to be done by me, and that was terrifying. I wasn't educated in the law. I didn't have the skills or the knowledge to navigate the complex legal system on my own. And that was scary—not in the way that you're afraid of something jumping out at you, but in a deep, paralyzing way where you know you're out of your depth.

How was I supposed to build a defense for myself? How was I supposed to find the right arguments, the right precedents, the right motions to file? It felt like trying to climb a mountain without any gear, without a map, without even knowing where the summit was. And all the while, I was acutely aware of the stakes. This wasn't just about winning or losing. This was my life.

When I read that "Dear John" letter from the attorney, it knocked the wind out of me. It was like being dropped into a pit with no way out. But even then, even in my lowest moments, there was still a fight in me. I couldn't give up. I knew that this was going to take time, and I had to be prepared for the long haul. I had to keep believing that one day, the truth would come out, and justice would be served.

Despite everything, I wasn't alone. There were people who believed in me, who believed in my story, who believed in my innocence. They knew who I was. They knew I wasn't capable of taking a life. Their faith in me kept me going when my own faith wavered. They gave me a reason to keep fighting, a reason to keep pushing forward, no matter how hard it got.

In those moments of despair, I felt a glimmer of something more than just existence. I felt like a living soul, like there was still a part of me that was alive and burning with the desire for justice. I clung to that feeling, to that small, flickering flame of hope. It was all I had, and I wasn't going to let it go. Not now. Not ever.

Deon's Thoughts

Here we are now, two years after the fight for justice began in earnest, and the hope that once felt so distant is starting to feel within reach. I remember that day like it was yesterday. I was sitting in my cell, counting the days—like I'd been doing for years—when a guard handed me a copy of the Chicago Tribune. The headline read, "New Doubts Cast on Verdict; Inmate Disputes Guilt of 4 Others Convicted of '92 Double Murder."

It was like the universe had thrown me a lifeline. I sat down on the edge of my bed, the newspaper trembling in my hands. My eyes raced over the words, devouring each sentence, each paragraph, with a hunger I hadn't felt in years. This article wasn't just news—it was a spotlight on the cracks in the walls that had held me captive for over a decade.

We were actually in court, fighting not just for our freedom but for our lives, for our names. This wasn't just about overturning a wrongful conviction; it was about vindicating the truth. We had cast doubt on our verdicts—real doubt. And that doubt, that sliver of uncertainty, was what we were clinging to. Because in that doubt lay the possibility of freedom.

A Ray of Light in the Darkness

As I read, I felt something stirring inside me, something I hadn't allowed myself to feel for a long time: hope. Real, tangible hope. Not the fragile, fleeting kind that fades as quickly as it comes, but the kind that digs in deep and takes root in your soul. The kind of hope that reminds you why you're still fighting, why you've held on this long.

This article—it brought a little better light into the dark place where we had been for so long. It was a small beacon, but it was enough to make us believe that maybe, just maybe, this was finally coming to an end. I could almost taste the air outside these prison walls, feel the warmth of the sun on my face, hear the sounds of the city that had once been my home.

But more than that, it made me feel like I wasn't invisible. Like the world outside these bars hadn't forgotten about me, about us. Someone out there was listening, someone cared enough to write about our fight, to tell our story. And that mattered. It mattered more than I can even put into words.

The days that followed were filled with a renewed sense of purpose. We weren't just inmates anymore—we were men on the brink of freedom, on the cusp of reclaiming the lives that had been stolen from us. We were starting to believe, truly believe, that this nightmare was finally coming to an end.

That article was more than just words on a page; it was a reminder that the truth has a way of coming to light, no matter how deep it's buried. And in that moment, sitting in my cell with that newspaper in my hands, I knew that we were closer than ever to seeing that light shine on us.

Chapter 14

The Roller Coaster

Daniel's Thoughts

March 19, 2003. I remember that date as if it were etched into my very being. Steve Mills and Maurice Possley—names that had become synonymous with hope in my struggle—had penned another article about my case. The headline screamed, "'92 Murder Conviction Stands Despite New Evidence," and with each word, I felt the ground beneath me tremble. It was as if the entire weight of the world had been dumped onto my shoulders, threatening to crush me beneath its enormity.

CHICAGO TRIBUNE: '92 murder conviction stands despite new evidence

March 19, 2003

By Steve Mills and Maurice Possley

Cook County prosecutors said Tuesday they are unconvinced by new information suggesting four men were wrongly convicted of a 1992 double murder, including one man who, records showed, was being held in a police lockup when the crime occurred.

Daniel Taylor and four other men were convicted of the Nov. 16, 1992, murders of Jeffrey Lassiter, 41, and Sharon Haugabook, 37, inside a North Side apartment.

The Roller Coaster

The five men, as well as three others, confessed to the crimes and implicated each other, though arrest and bond records showed Taylor had been under arrest and was not released until after the murders were committed--making it impossi-ble for him to be involved and raising questions about all the confessions.

A Tribune investigation in December 2001 and a follow-up in January 2003 uncovered additional information suggest-ing that Taylor and at least three others had been wrongly convicted.

In addition to Taylor, four others in the case are in prison--Dennis Mixon, Lewis Gardner, Deon Patrick and Paul Phil-lips. Taylor, Mixon and Patrick are serving life sentences at Stateville Correctional Center. Gardner and Phillips are serving 30-year sentences at Danville Correctional Center.

Mixon told the Tribune late last year that his co-defendants had nothing to do with the murders and that he identified one of two men he says he brought to Lassiter's apartment and who were involved.

Mixon provided the same account to prosecutors last week.

"Nothing has changed," said John Gorman, spokesman for State's Atty. Richard Devine. "Whatever we've uncovered thus far has not resulted in a change in the status of the case. [Taylor] remains convicted."

The state's attorney's office investigation continues.

Last year, Willie Triplett told the Tribune he was outside the apartment building when the murders occurred and saw Mixon leave the building before the shots were fired. He said Taylor and the others were not involved.

Triplett said Tuesday he recently told an investigator from the state's attorney's office the same story and offered to tes-tify.

"I told him that I didn't see the murder, but I saw them come out," he said. "I told them the same thing I said before--that's how it happened. Those guys are innocent. I am willing to do something about it."

Kathleen Zellner, who represents Taylor and his co-defendants, said it was critical for prosecutors to continue pursuing their reinvestigation of the case.

"This is a case where the people in jail are clearly innocent," said Zellner. "Even though we don't have DNA, it's incum-bent on the defense and

the prosecution to continue to investigate this. They've got an opinion on this, and it's that we don't yet have enough evidence."

Taylor said he does not understand why prosecutors cannot see that he and his co-defendants were not involved in the double murder.

"I don't know why it's so hard to get me out, for them to understand I didn't do this," Taylor said Tuesday in a telephone interview. "I don't know why they can't see this."

Daniel's Feedback

When the article hit the newsstands, it was like a punch to the gut. I read the words over and over, trying to make sense of them. It felt as though every shred of hope I had clung to was being yanked away, leaving me grappling with a stark, brutal reality. I was in a relentless dogfight with the State of Chicago's attorneys—a fight where every attempt to present evidence of my innocence was met with a firm, unyielding wall of denial. This moment wasn't just another setback; it was a devastating blow that cut deeper than I had anticipated.

The realization that the state was not only dismissing the evidence but actively refusing to reconsider my case was almost too much to bear. Each denial felt like a personal affront, an aggressive assertion that my pleas for justice were unworthy of consideration. The sense of betrayal was profound, like being stranded in a foreign land with no hope of return, facing an accusation that was as alien as it was unjust.

To describe the feeling of loss in this situation is challenging—words seem to fall short of capturing the depth of the anguish. It was more than just emotional pain; it was an assault on my spirit. Imagine being imprisoned in another country for a crime you didn't commit, cut off from your life and loved ones, with every attempt to prove your innocence dismissed. This feeling, this profound despair, is what consumed me as I grappled with the news of yet another petition being denied by the very system that was supposed to deliver justice.

The persistent denial by the judicial system was not just a legal setback; it was a personal blow, a constant reminder of how far I was from the truth being recognized. The emotions I felt were a whirlwind of frustration, sadness, and hopelessness, each one intertwining with the others in a chaotic dance of despair. It was a dark moment, one where every bit of progress seemed to dissolve into nothingness, leaving me with nothing but the cold reality of my situation.

In the face of this overwhelming sense of loss, I was left to navigate the stormy seas of my emotions, clinging to the faint hope that somewhere, somehow, justice would eventually prevail.

Deon's Thoughts

March 19, 2003: The day started like any other—waking up to the cold reality of prison life, the bars, the routine, the heavy weight of time pressing down on me. But there was something different in the air, a tension that lingered as I made my way to the common area. It had been 78 days since our last court date, 78 days of holding on to whatever sliver of hope I could find.

I remember the whispers spreading through the hallways like wildfire. "Did you hear? The Tribune's running a story on our case today." My stomach twisted. I could feel the anticipation building, that uneasy mix of hope and dread that I'd become all too familiar with over the years. Every time there was news, it felt like I was standing on the edge of a cliff, waiting to see if I'd be pushed off or pulled back.

When I finally got my hands on the paper, my heart pounded so hard I could barely breathe. The headline read, "'92 Murder Conviction Stands Despite New Evidence." My vision blurred for a second, and I had to read it twice to make sure I wasn't imagining things.

How could this be happening? We had new evidence—solid, undeniable proof that should have turned the case on its head. The kind of evidence that should've set us free, sent us back to our families, to our lives that had been ripped away. But there it was in black and white, plain as day: "Conviction Stands."

I slumped down onto the nearest bench, the paper crumpling in my hands as I gripped it tightly. The words felt like a punch to the gut. How many times have we been here? So close, just within reach of justice, only to have it yanked away at the last second. I felt like I was on a never-ending roller coaster, the highs getting fewer and the lows sinking even deeper.

I could feel the eyes of the other inmates on me, some of them sharing in my despair, others too numb to care anymore. It wasn't just me who was crushed by this. We had all been riding this roller coaster together, all of us clinging to the hope that maybe this time things would be different. Maybe this time, someone would finally see the truth.

But hope is a strange thing. Even as I sat there, feeling like my world had crumbled all over again, I couldn't let go of it entirely. It's like a stubborn flame that refuses to die, even when the wind keeps trying to snuff it out. Deep down, I knew we couldn't give up, no matter how many times we got knocked down. If we gave up, we'd be letting them win. We'd be letting the system crush us entirely. So, we picked ourselves up. We kept going. We kept fighting, because what else could we do? Giving up wasn't an option. Not for me, not for any of us. We had to keep pushing forward, keep believing that one day, somehow, justice would be ours.

Later that month, the Chicago Tribune released an article on March 30, 2012, titled "Strong Proof He's Innocent: More Documents Indicate That Inmate Was in a Police Lockup When 1992 Double Murder Occurred," The article wasn't directly related to our case, but it raised awareness on how the justice system was seemingly trying to fix the errors in their interrogation process. I came across another piece that stirred a mix of emotions within me. This new article reported that the State's Attorney's Office was starting to train their prosecutors to identify false confessions. The headline alone felt like a small victory, a sign that maybe, just maybe, things were shifting.

Reading about the initiative to educate prosecutors on recognizing false confessions was both reassuring and frustrating. It was reassuring because it signaled a potential change in the system—a system that had wronged so many of us. It was frustrating because, while this training was a step in the right direction, it did nothing to address the pain and injustice we had endured. The article was a beacon of hope for those who might find themselves in similar situations in the future, but it did nothing to rectify the wrongs that had already been committed against us.

As I read through the article, I couldn't help but feel a twinge of

The Roller Coaster

hope. It was a glimmer, a small acknowledgment that the tactics and torture we had faced were recognized as problematic. Knowing that someone in power was paying attention, that there was a recognition of the wrongs in those interrogation rooms, was a small comfort. It was as if a faint light had flickered in the dark tunnel we had been navigating for so long. However, this newfound hope was tempered by a stark reality. The article did nothing to change our current predicament. It didn't free us from the cages of our wrongful convictions. It didn't undo the psychological and emotional damage we had endured. It was a reminder that while progress might be on the horizon, it had yet to reach us.

What truly struck me was how the articles continued to highlight our stories, to shed light on our struggles, but they did so without bringing tangible relief. Our supporters and advocates, the ones pushing for justice on our behalf, were still fighting the good fight, still amplifying our voices. Their efforts were crucial, but they couldn't change the past or instantly fix our present.

Despite the article's shortcomings in directly helping us, it did offer a modicum of solace. It reminded us that we were not alone, that our experiences were not in vain, and that there were those out there who understood and were working to make sure that future generations wouldn't suffer as we had. It wasn't much, but in a world where progress often felt agonizingly slow, any sign of change was a small victory in itself.

Chapter 15

The Crushing Weight of Denial

Daniel's Thoughts

April 2, 2003, was supposed to be just another day in my life—a day filled with the same relentless cycle of waiting and hoping. But that day, the Chicago Tribune published an article titled "When the Obvious Isn't Enough," and it cut through the monotony of my imprisonment with an unsettling clarity.

I remember the moment I read the article. It was a mix of disbelief and disillusionment. The piece detailed Cook County State's Attorney Richard Devine's efforts to train prosecutors to recognize false confessions and prevent wrongful convictions. It was supposed to be a sign of progress, a glimmer of hope that things were changing, that the justice system was finally acknowledging its flaws and taking steps to correct them.

CHICAGO TRIBUNE: When the obvious isn't enough
April 2, 2003

To his credit, Cook County State's Atty. Richard Devine has started training his prosecutors on how to watch out for instances where suspects might falsely confess to crimes. Conducted by Chief Deputy State's Atty.

The Crushing Weight of Denial

Robert Milan, the seminars focus on recognizing when overzealous investigations lead to wrongful convictions.

Apparently it's not all that hard to extract a bogus confession, no matter how strong-willed or self-assured the suspect appears to be. Usually it takes a combination of intimidation, exhaustion and suggestion. In some cases, physical coer-cion has provided a speedier inducement.

Despite a mounting number of cases in which DNA evidence proves that innocent people have confessed, juries still have a hard time believing anyone would admit to a crime he didn't commit. Thankfully, Cook County prosecutors now will be better prepared as a first line of defense against wrongful convictions.

That's very welcome news. But it also makes it all the more mysterious that county prosecutors have yet applied the lessons learned to a glaring case in their own shop.

Daniel Taylor has been living behind bars for a decade, ever since he was convicted of a double murder and sentenced to life in prison.

Records, however, show that he was in jail at the time the murders occurred.

That thorny little fact hasn't so far been convincing enough for prosecutors to admit they might have made a grave mis-take.

The Cook County state's attorney's office says it has been looking into this claim for more than 15 months, when new evidence uncovered by Tribune reporters Steve Mills and Maurice Possley, along with former Tribune reporter Ken Armstrong, was published. They call it a "top priority" for the office. But so far their lengthy investigation has yielded no conclusions.

At the time of the murders, Taylor was 17. He had lived much of his life in foster homes, and at the time of his arrest essentially lived on the streets and belonged to a gang.

He was also young, suggestible and easily worn down by police.

Police arrest reports show that Taylor was locked up for disorderly conduct at 6:45 p.m. on Nov. 16, 1992, the night of the murders. Bond slips show he wasn't released until 10 p.m.

The murders occurred at 8:43 p.m., police said.

But that didn't stop investigators from building a case against Taylor.

They found a witness who testified he saw Taylor a block or two away at a park about 7:30 that night. But that witness, who happened to be a rival gang member and who got leniency on a narcotics charge, later said he lied at the request of detectives.

Then two patrolmen filed a report--a month late--saying they saw Taylor on the street near the murder site. But the chronology they gave didn't square with facts later uncovered by the Tribune. And one of the officers had dubious credibility; four months earlier, in an unrelated case, a Cook County circuit court judge threw him off the witness stand, calling him a "liar."

No physical evidence connected Taylor to the crime.

Devine has recently made several good efforts to restore confidence in the criminal justice system through legislation and better practices in his office. He also should be more aggressive about concluding the questions around the Daniel Taylor case.

Granted, it's complicated; seven other people also confessed to taking part in the murders. They all implicated each other, including Taylor, which raises serious questions about the validity of all the confessions. Another man serving a life sentence for the crime, Dennis Mixon, says he took part in the crime with a person who was never charged with these murders. Mixon also says he had never even met any of his "co-conspirators" until he went to jail.

Devine has had more than a year to investigate, and now has the benefit of heightened awareness about the possibility of false confessions. That should be more than enough to settle for good all the nagging doubts that plague this case.

Daniel's Feedback

As I read through the article, I couldn't shake the feeling that it was all just smoke and mirrors. Devine's so-called reforms felt like nothing more than lip service—a superficial gesture meant to placate public concern rather than address the root issues that led to my wrongful conviction. I couldn't help but think that this was merely a well-crafted PR move, designed to make it look like they were doing something about the very problems that had unjustly imprisoned me for over a decade.

The article made a point of explaining how easy it was to extract false confessions through a mix of intimidation, exhaustion, and suggestion. It described how even the most resolute suspects could be worn down and coerced into admitting to crimes they didn't commit. It was a textbook explanation of what I had experienced firsthand. I knew all too well the methods used to break me down during those interrogations in December 1992. I had been young, vulnerable, and utterly at the mercy of overzealous police officers who seemed more interested in closing a case than uncovering the truth.

Yet, the article failed to make any meaningful connection to my case. It was as if the acknowledgment of the problem was enough, without any real intent to apply these insights to rectify the mistakes made in my conviction. I saw it as a way to soothe public outrage without making any genuine effort to confront the systemic issues at play.

I felt that Richard Devine and his office were merely going through the motions. While they publicly acknowledged the flaws in their interrogation practices, there was no tangible indication that they were taking concrete steps to address these issues in my case. The article, to me, seemed like a calculated move to show that they were aware of the problem but lacked the courage or commitment to face it head-on.

Reading about these supposed reforms only deepened my frustration. It was a stark reminder that while the world outside was supposedly evolving, the grim reality of my situation remained unchanged. The acknowledgment of the problem was hollow and meaningless without real action. I couldn't help but think that the article did little more than provide a facade of progress, masking the lack of real accountability and justice.

As I sat in my cell, grappling with the implications of the Tribune's piece, I couldn't escape the sense of disillusionment. It felt as though the system was more interested in protecting its own image than in correcting its grave mistakes. The article had done nothing to alleviate my suffering or bring me any closer to the justice I desperately sought. It was, in the end, a reminder that in the world of wrongful convictions, acknowledging the problem was not the same as solving it.

Deon's Thoughts

A couple of weeks after the article "When the Obvious Isn't Enough" was published on April 2, 2003, I remember feeling a mix of frustration and faint hope. The piece highlighted the Cook County State's Attorney's Office's new initiative to train their prosecutors to recognize false confessions. They were finally acknowledging the problems we had been shouting about for years—the tactics of intimidation, exhaustion, and suggestion that led us to falsely admit to crimes we didn't commit.

For us, sitting in our cells, the article was both a faint indication and a painful reminder of our own ongoing struggles. The thought that prosecutors were being trained to spot false confessions brought a slight reprieve to our beaten spirits. It was as if someone, somewhere, was beginning to understand the grave mistakes made in those interrogation rooms. It was comforting to know that the very tactics used against us were now being scrutinized, that someone in power was finally taking notice.

But, that small sign was quickly overshadowed by the reality of our situation. While the article was a sign that things might change for future suspects, it did nothing to alter our own dire circumstances. We were still behind bars, still battling against the convictions that were based on coerced confessions and flawed investigations. The article seemed to serve more as a nod to the ongoing issues within the justice system rather than a direct lifeline for those of us who were trapped by its failings.

Even as the article's message provided some solace, it was bittersweet. We had been through the wringer, and while others might benefit from these new practices, our fights were still very much alive. The people who supported us and fought tirelessly for our release were the ones who kept pushing forward, highlighting our cases and advocating for change. The article was another step towards acknowledging the wrongs, but for us, it was a stark reminder of the slow, painful journey towards justice.

So, while the article did offer a sliver of hope, it was clear that much more needed to be done. It wasn't enough to change our reality, but it was a sign that the system might eventually correct itself. We could only

The Crushing Weight of Denial

hope that these changes would come soon enough to save others from the same fate we had endured.

Chapter 16

The Tide Turns

Daniel's Thoughts

April 18, 2003, was a day that I had been waiting for, with a mixture of hope and trepidation. I remember picking up the newspaper and seeing the headline: "Alibi Offered for Convict in Killings; Lawyer: Case is 'Fatally Flawed.'" My heart skipped a beat as I read through the article, trying to absorb every detail, hoping for a sign that the truth was finally starting to break through the surface.

The article reported that Mark Tillis, a man serving a sentence for burglary, had come forward with an alibi for Paul Phillips, one of my co-defendants. Tillis claimed that on the night of November 16, 1992, he was with Phillips, playing video games at Phillips' mother's apartment. According to Tillis, Phillips couldn't have been the lookout during the murders because he was with him during that crucial time. This was significant because Phillips had been convicted of acting as a lookout while the murders were being committed.

CHICAGO TRIBUNE: News story: Alibi offered for convict in killings; Lawyer: Case is 'fatally flawed'
April 18, 2003
By Steve Mills and Maurice Possley,

The Tide Turns

As Cook County prosecutors near the end of a reinvestigation of the convictions of five men for a double murder in 1992, another witness has come forward to provide an alibi for one of the men.

Mark Tillis, who is serving a 3-year sentence for burglary, said in an interview at the Downstate Pinckneyville Correc-tional Center that he was in an apartment playing video games with Paul Phillips at the time of the Nov. 16, 1992, slay-ings.

Phillips is serving a 30-year prison term after being convicted of acting as a lookout while the murders were committed.

"Paul was with me and I [can't] see how he was doing a lookout," Tillis said.

The state's attorney's office began investigating the convictions of Phillips and four other men after a Tribune article raised questions about whether they were wrongly convicted, even though police said all of them had confessed to par-ticipating in the crime.

Kathleen Zellner, an attorney who now represents the defendants, said prosecutors had informed her they would soon make a decision on whether to reopen the case.

"It's clear the case is fatally flawed," Zellner said. "This witness is just another part of the evidence that shows a mistake has been made and this was a miscarriage of justice."

Convicted along with Phillips were Daniel Taylor, Deon Patrick, Lewis Gardner and Dennis Mixon. Taylor, Mixon and Patrick were sentenced to life in prison, and Gardner is serving a 30-year term.

They were convicted of killing Jeffrey Lassiter, 41, and Sharon Haugabook, 37, in an apartment at 910 W. Agatite Ave.

The five men, as well as three others, confessed to the crimes and impli-cated each other. But arrest and bond records show Taylor had been under arrest and was not released until after the murders were committed.

Police reports show Taylor was locked up for disorderly conduct at 6:45 p.m. on the night of the murders. A bond slip showed that he was not released from the Town Hall District lockup until 10 p.m.

The murders occurred at 8:43 p.m., according to police.

A Tribune investigation in December 2001 and a follow-up in January 2003 uncovered information suggesting that Tay-lor, Phillips, Patrick and Gardner had been wrongly convicted.

A drug dealer who testified that he saw Taylor on the street at 7:30 p.m. told the Tribune he lied at the request of detec-tives. Documents and interviews undermined a report by two police officers, filed weeks after authorities learned of Taylor's jail records, that they saw him on the street at 9:30 p.m. that night.

Another witness, never before interviewed by police, told the Tribune he was outside the apartment building when the murders occurred and saw Mixon leave the building before the shots were fired. He said Taylor and the others were not involved.

In an interview at Stateville Correctional Center, Mixon said he went to the building with two other men to collect money from Lassiter and fled from the building just before the fatal shots were fired. He said Taylor, Phillips and the other co-defendants had nothing to do with the murders and he had never even met them until he was arrested in the case.

Mixon has identified for prosecutors one of the two men he said he brought to Lassiter's apartment.

Tillis said that on the night of the murders, he was with Paul Phillips at Phillips' mother's apartment. He disputed the prosecution's assertion that Phillips was with his co-defendants at a gang meeting in nearby Clarendon Park and then acted as a lookout for the killers.

Shortly after the murders, police responding to the scene said they saw Tillis, then 16, in an alley near the building where Haugabook and Lassiter were killed. They said they chased him into the Phillips' apartment. There, police said, they arrested Phillips' mother on a narcotics possession charge and took Tillis into custody because he was interfering with the arrest of Phillips' mother.

But in the interview, Tillis, who is now 27, said he was not the one police chased into the apartment--that he was al-ready there and had been there much of the day. He said police had actually chased Phillips' brother, Akia, into the apartment.

He said that after being arrested, he was taken to a police station and later released to the custody of his mother. Tillis said he never returned to the neighborhood and never saw Paul or Akia Phillips again. He said he was never called as a witness in Paul Phillips' trial.

Tillis said he recently was interviewed by an investigator for the state's

The Tide Turns

attorney's office and gave the same account of Phillips' whereabouts that day.

John Gorman, spokesman for the state's attorney's office, said Tillis gave a different account to the investigator. Gorman said the investigator reported that Tillis said police had chased Paul, not Akia, Phillips into the apartment after 10 p.m. Gorman said the police report showed that the arrest occurred more than an hour before 10 p.m.

In addition, Gorman said Paul Phillips, when he was interviewed recently by a state's attorney's investigator, did not recall being in the apartment and said he was at a girlfriend's house at the time of the crime.

"We have a team of people working on this," Gorman said. "It is a priority, and we are continuing our investigation."

Daniel's Feedback

I felt a rush of relief as I read that the state was beginning to question the validity of our convictions. The article mentioned that the state's attorney's office was considering reopening the case. For the first time in years, I felt a weight lift from my shoulders. It wasn't the entire burden of my wrongful conviction, but it was enough to make me feel lighter, even if just for a moment.

Reading the details of Tillis' statement, I felt a comforting prospect. The idea that someone was finally challenging the flawed narrative that had been used to convict us was a breath of fresh air. It was as if a crack had appeared in the wall that had been holding us captive in a lie. I knew it wasn't a guarantee of freedom, but it was a start—a sign that the truth might be closer to coming out.

The road to justice was far from over, and I was acutely aware of the lengthy journey that lay ahead. Even with this new development, it would still take another ten years before I would finally be freed from the chains of a wrongful conviction. But at that moment, the publication of that article gave me a sense of renewed determination. It reminded me that there were people out there who were willing to fight for the truth, and that sometimes, the most unexpected sources could bring the clarity needed to challenge the injustices we faced.

The battle to prove our innocence was filled with ups and downs, with every small victory bringing its own set of challenges. The emotional toll of fighting for justice was immense, but each bit of new evidence or supportive statement provided a glimmer of hope, reinforcing my resolve to keep pushing forward.

Reading that article was a turning point, a reminder that despite the long road ahead, we were making progress. It was a testament to the fact that even in the darkest times, there was always a chance for light to break through. And as I continued to fight, knowing that others were fighting alongside me and that our story was finally being heard, I held onto that hope, even when the path seemed endless.

Deon's Thoughts

I remember the day I got my hands on the Chicago Tribune article like it was yesterday. It was April 18, 2003. I was sitting on the edge of my cot, the same cot where I had spent countless nights wrestling with the demons of despair, trying to hold on to a shred of hope. But this day felt different. There was an electricity in the air that I couldn't quite explain.

When the guard slid the newspaper under my cell door, my hands trembled as I picked it up. The headline leaped off the page: "Alibi Offered for Convict in Killings; Lawyer: Case is 'Fatally Flawed'" by Steve Mills and Maurice Possley. My heart pounded in my chest as I read the first few lines.

This was it. This was what I had been waiting for, what I had been praying for during all those long nights. The evidence was finally starting to take shape. Real evidence. Not the twisted, manufactured nonsense that had put me behind bars, but the truth—something that could actually set me free.

The article detailed how, after years of being silenced, witnesses were coming forward. They were speaking up, telling the truth about where I was the night of those murders. These were people who had nothing to gain, nothing to lose, just a desire to see justice done. They knew, and now the world would know, that I couldn't have possibly been at the scene of the crime. I was somewhere else entirely.

I couldn't believe it at first. The words felt surreal, like I was dreaming and any moment I would wake up back in the nightmare I

The Tide Turns

had been living for so long. But as I read on, the reality of it all began to sink in. This was real. Finally, after so many years, the truth was coming to light.

Steve Mills and Maurice Possley were the heroes I didn't even know I had. They took this story, this painful, twisted story, and they ran with it. They didn't just report it; they fought for it. They fought for me. The article mentioned how they had been gathering momentum, not just finding witnesses but putting together the facts—facts that could dismantle the case against me.

The article also highlighted a chilling detail: this was happening just two weeks after the prosecutors had been trained in tactics for extracting false confessions. It was as if the timing was some kind of sick joke, a cruel twist in a story that had already taken so much from me. But this time, the joke was on them. Because with each witness that came forward, with each piece of evidence that was uncovered, their case was crumbling. They knew it, and I knew it.

As I sat there in my cell, the weight of the article pressed down on me, but it was a different kind of weight. It wasn't the suffocating despair I had felt for so long. This was the weight of hope, of possibility, of a future that had seemed so distant finally creeping closer.

I folded the newspaper and held it to my chest, closing my eyes. For the first time in years, I allowed myself to imagine a life beyond these walls. A life where I wasn't defined by the number on my prison uniform but by the person I was, the person I had always been.

That day marked a turning point, not just in my case but in my life. The truth was finally coming out, and with it, the possibility of freedom. Steve Mills and Maurice Possley had lit a fire, and there was no putting it out now. The tide was turning, and for the first time in a long time, I felt like I might just ride that wave all the way to freedom.

Chapter 17

Flickers Of Possibility

Daniel's Thoughts

June 23, 2003, was a day that turned my world upside down in ways I hadn't anticipated. On that day, an article titled "When to Own Up to Mistakes" was published, and reading it felt like I was strapped into a roller coaster, hurtling through a whirlwind of emotions. The article spoke to something deep within me—an urgent call for accountability and truth. It was a beacon of hope that the wrongs committed against me and seven other innocent men might finally be acknowledged. Yet, as much as the article's message resonated with me, it also stirred a profound sense of dread.

CHICAGO TRIBUNE: Editorial: When to own up to mistakes
June 23, 2003

In California, a young attorney named Alison Tucher worked doggedly the last four years to convince prosecutors that a man they imprisoned 12 years ago for murder was innocent.

Working pro bono, Tucher interviewed witnesses in prison, pored over trial transcripts and found holes in the case. She linked fingerprints at the crime scene to the real killer, figured out how he had framed Rick Walker, then unearthed receipts that supported Walker's alibi.

Flickers Of Possibility

A few days ago, prosecutors agreed with her.

The Santa Clara County district attorney not only agreed that Walker was innocent, he did something astonishing. He congratulated and praised Tucher for her work, immediately released the inmate and promised to assist him after his release. In an emotional meeting, a veteran prosecutor from the office apologized personally to the man.

And then, there is Cook County.

Here, prosecutors have refused to acknowledge obvious errors made in three separate cases by the Cook County state's attorney's office and Chicago police.

Two men whose convictions rested on the testimony of a discredited witness were released recently by order of a judge. The judge signaled he has serious doubts about the quality of the case, particularly because it has since been under-minded by DNA evidence. Yet assistants to Cook County State's Atty. Richard Devine says they plan nonetheless to retry the men.

Six men continue to serve lengthy sentences for convictions that are based on questionable and tainted evidence. New DNA evidence in two of those cases buttresses the longstanding claim that the imprisoned men did not commit the crimes of which they were convicted.

Combined, the eight men in these cases have spent more than a century in prison, yet the cases against them are so weak the slightest touch has them flaking apart like pie crust.

Daniel Taylor has spent more than a decade behind bars for a double murder--but records show he was in a police dis-trict lockup at the time of the crime. Those records also cast doubt about the validity of confessions made by Taylor and by three co-defendants who say Taylor committed the murder with them. All are serving lengthy sentences.

A credible eyewitness at the scene said Taylor was a familiar face in the neighborhood, but insisted he was not one of the men that she saw walk out of the building right after the shooting. She did, however, identify one man who later told Tribune reporters he was involved in the crime with three others, but not with Taylor or any of the three men serving time for it. He has told prosecutors varying stories.

The murders occurred at 8:43 p.m. But police records show Taylor was arrested for causing a street disturbance at 6:45 p.m. that night--an event he remembered only after his confession. The 17-year-old was transported to the police station at 6:55 p.m. He was received into the lockup at 7:25 p.m. Charges were approved at 9:45 p.m. His bond slip shows he was released at 10 p.m.

It's an enormous stretch to think that five different police officers who were responsible for jotting down or signing off on those times all were off by a matter of hours.

But prosecutors aren't bothered by that.

They prefer instead to rely on the story of two officers who said they saw Taylor walking a few blocks from the murder site around 9:30 p.m. Their report was filed a month after this supposed encounter. In an unrelated case not long before Taylor's, one of those officers was dismissed from the witness stand by a judge who found him lacking in credibility and who called him a "liar."

In closing argument at trial, the prosecutors carefully chose which police paperwork to believe. One asserted, "paper-work is not foolproof. But I'll tell you what is foolproof. And what is foolproof are the defendant's own words."

The jury bought it.

We know much more today than we did a decade ago about confessions. We know that many times DNA evidence has refuted a "confession" by a defendant. We know that young and mentally impaired suspects in particular can be swayed, or coerced, into giving false confessions. The defendant's own words are not always foolproof.

Devine knows this well. Earlier this year he started holding seminars to train his prosecutors on how to look out for false confessions.

Yet prosecutors in the office remain unconvinced that Taylor is innocent of murder. And the jail records? "There are plenty of police documents that are challenged at trial," said a spokesman for Devine.

Prosecutors have been re-investigating this case for 18 months. They have yet to re-interview Daniel Taylor, who has professed his innocence for more than a decade.

Not another penny of taxpayer money should be wasted on perpetuating the injustice of keeping Taylor behind bars. It's time to focus on who really killed Jeffrey Lassiter and Sharon Haugabook on Nov. 16, 1992.

It's time to let Daniel Taylor go.

Flickers Of Possibility

Three men implicated themselves and each other in confessions to the 1990 rape and strangulation of Kathy Morgan.

Harold Hill was 16 at the time of the crime, 18 when he confessed to it. Dan Young Jr. had an IQ of 56, far below the borderline for mental retardation, when he confessed. Young was unable to state where the sun rises or what a ship is, according to two psychiatrists and a psychologist. He was incapable of writing anything but his name.

Shortly after making their statements, Hill and Young asserted that their confessions had been coerced. A third defen-dant, Peter Williams, lends credibility to that claim.

Williams confessed to the same crime. He confessed in far greater detail, and he implicated Hill and Young, just as Hill and Young had implicated him. One problem: Jail records showed that Williams had been locked up at the time of the murder, casting doubt on all three confessions. This time prosecutors didn't dispute the records. Williams was released.

Williams later said his confession was coerced. He said he was handcuffed to a radiator for hours and forced to urinate on himself because police wouldn't let him use the washroom.

DNA testing on hairs found at the murder scene excluded Hill and Young. DNA material taken from the victim's fin-gernail did not match that of Hill or Young. In a rather far-fetched argument, prosecutors speculate that police or paramedics could have left sweat or drool on the woman's fingernails.

A judge has given Hill and Young a chance to make their case next month for a new trial. Prosecutors oppose a new trial. "There are people who are always trying to get out of their confession," said Devine's spokesman.

Then there's the case of Michael Evans and Paul Terry, who served more than 25 years in prison for the abduction, rape and murder of 9-year-old Lisa Cabassa.

Their conviction rests on the testimony of one key eyewitness, someone who changed her story repeatedly and admitted on the stand that she had lied to police about what she knew.

The woman waited days after the crime before contacting officers with her information that she saw three men strug-gling with a girl on the street. Prosecutors excuse her delay with the argument that she felt threatened. But the woman was a close friend of the wife of the lead investigator on the case. Which raises the question: If she felt threatened, would she not have called that friend--instead of calling a $5,000 reward hotline set up in the wake of the crime?

Recent DNA testing of a semen swab taken from the victim has excluded Evans and Terry, as well as every other per-son Chicago police detectives once implicated as accomplices.

Evans and Terry were released last month by a Cook County judge. Nevertheless, prosecutors plan to retry them. Prose-cutors acknowledge the case has a few pockmarks, but they believe that they have sufficient evidence to reconvict both men. "We still have an eyewitness who is very strong," said the prosecutors' spokesman. "She is adamant about what she saw."

In this instance, too, we know far more today about the fallibility of eyewitness identification than we did when the case was first tried. Acknowledging new research showing mistaken eyewitness identification is the most common problem behind wrongful convictions, the Illinois legislature recently voted to prohibit death sentences for those who are con-victed on the testimony of a single eyewitness.

We are able to test DNA material left behind at a crime scene in a way that yields more precise results than in the past. And the person who, again, should know this better than anyone is Richard Devine.

Prosecutors have an obligation to pursue the truth. They are given wide discretion in deciding what cases to bring to trial based on the evidence available to them. They are not paid to splash after-shave on a stinker case and hope for a win from the jury.

New information may not have proven that all these defendants are innocent, but it has at the very least cast overwhelm-ing doubt about guilt. Moreover, it has created deep suspicions that these cases were tainted by coerced confessions and selective evaluation of the evidence that was available.

It is time for Richard Devine to use his prosecutor's discretion and end these cases immediately. He needs to consider the evidence that grave mistakes were made; he should investigate them and correct them.

And then attention can turn to a task that has been ignored for far too long in these cases: Finding--and punishing--the real killers.

Flickers Of Possibility

Daniel's Feedback

The idea of the system admitting its errors and owning up to the wrongful convictions was both exhilarating and terrifying. On one hand, I felt a surge of hope that justice might finally be served. The article articulated something I had been yearning to hear—a recognition of the systemic failures that led to my unjust imprisonment. It was a validation that what I had endured was not just a personal tragedy but a systemic issue that needed addressing.

But that exhilaration came with a heavy price. Exposing the system's flaws, especially in a way that demanded accountability, is a dangerous endeavor. I knew that the state, when threatened, could be ruthless in its retaliation. Even though I was already serving a life sentence plus 230 years, my fear wasn't about physical harm. I had come to terms with the fact that my body was confined; my spirit, however, was still free and fighting.

The real fear was that the state could use its power to ensure that I remained trapped within their system. They had the means to manipulate and prolong my suffering, to use every trick in their book to prevent me from proving my innocence and regaining my freedom. This realization was a heavy burden. I was terrified of the potential consequences of challenging such a formidable entity.

Despite this fear, something remarkable happened. My fear was overshadowed by the strength I drew from my unwavering belief in my innocence. The more I reflected on the article's message, the more resolute I became. I realized that I couldn't let the state's potential retaliation deter me from my quest for justice. They already had me in a position where I had nothing left to lose. My situation was dire, but my spirit was unyielding.

I had to push forward, not just for myself, but for the others who had been wrongfully convicted alongside me. The strength I found in my own innocence was a powerful motivator. It compelled me to keep fighting, to not let fear paralyze me. The article gave me renewed energy and focus, and I resolved to use it to fuel my fight for justice.

Reading that article was a pivotal moment. It confirmed my belief that the fight for truth was not only necessary but also worth every ounce of courage I could muster. It gave me the push I needed to overcome my fears and to continue my battle for freedom, knowing that I was on the right side of history.

In the end, the roller coaster of emotions I experienced that day became a catalyst for my determination. It was a reminder that even in the face of fear, the pursuit of justice and truth must prevail.

Deon's Thoughts

When I first laid eyes on the headline, "When to Own Up to Mistakes," in the Chicago Tribune, something inside me stirred—a flicker of hope, a sensation I'd almost forgotten existed. June 23, 2003, was just another day in a long string of days that blurred together, but this editorial changed everything. It was as if the universe had finally decided to shift in my favor, after years of pushing against me with relentless force.

The article didn't just talk about mistakes in general; it went straight to the heart of the matter—the State's Attorney's Office. It was a public call-out, a direct challenge to those who had held the power over our lives, who had taken my freedom with the cold indifference of a stamp on a file. The Tribune was putting the pressure where it belonged, right on the people who had wronged us, and for the first time, it felt like the truth was breaking through the cracks of their well-constructed lies.

As I read through the editorial, I felt a strange sense of vindication. They were finally being held accountable, even if it was just in the court of public opinion. The State's Attorney's Office was being forced to face the fact that they never really owned up to their mistakes. They never came out and said, "We were wrong." Instead, they always found a way to sidestep responsibility, hiding behind legal jargon like, "We just don't have enough evidence to retry them." It was a carefully crafted deflection, a way to save face without admitting fault.

But this time, it felt different. The Tribune was shining a light on their tactics, exposing the way they manipulated the narrative to avoid acknowledging the truth. And that truth was that I, and others like me, had been wrongfully convicted. We had been thrown into a system that was supposed to protect us, only to be chewed up and spit out by its machinery.

Flickers Of Possibility

Reading that article lit a fire in me. It was like someone had thrown gasoline on the embers of a nearly extinguished flame. I realized that we were putting the ball in their court, forcing them to answer for what they had done to us. They couldn't just sweep us under the rug anymore. The public was watching, and the pressure was mounting.

For so long, I had felt powerless, like a leaf caught in a raging river, being tossed around with no control over my own fate. But now, there was a shift. The article gave us momentum. It gave us a reason to keep fighting, to keep pushing for the truth to come out. It wasn't just about clearing my name anymore; it was about holding those in power accountable for their actions.

This wasn't just a battle for my freedom; it was a battle for justice. And reading that article, I felt a renewed sense of purpose. I knew the road ahead was still long and filled with obstacles, but for the first time in a long time, I felt like we had a chance. The fight wasn't over, and neither was I. That editorial was more than just words on a page—it was a lifeline, pulling me back from the edge of despair and reminding me that there was still hope.

Chapter 18

Still The Voiceless

Deon's Thoughts

Reading the Chicago Tribune's "Voice of the People" article was like stepping onto a roller coaster that I thought was finally about to take us to the top, only to be thrown back down again. As I read Richard A. Devine's response to the Tribune's June 23 editorial, I could feel a flicker of hope igniting within me. It was almost as if the words on the page were whispering promises of justice and change. For a brief moment, I allowed myself to believe that maybe, just maybe, something significant was about to happen in our case.

Devine's article was a mix of reassurance and deflection. He spoke about how they had dropped charges against those wrongfully convicted, like the four young men in the Lori Roscetti case and Corethian Bell, after DNA evidence proved their innocence. Hearing this made my heart race. Could our situation finally be on the verge of resolution? Was there a chance that the same diligence would be applied to our case?

CHICAGO TRIBUNE: VOICE OF THE PEOPLE "Ensuring that justice is done in Cook County"

Still The Voiceless

By Richard A. Devine, Cook County state's attorney Chicago
July 3, 2003

In its June 23 editorial, "When to own up to mistakes," the Tribune criticizes prosecutors for ignoring evidence of innocence in three old murder cases.

In recent years, however, we have not hesitated to drop cases when the evidence was not there.

We dropped charges against the four young men convicted in the 1986 slaying of Lori Roscetti after DNA results pointed away from the defendants. We dropped charges against Corethian Bell after similar evidence exonerated him.

While the editorial makes some legitimate points, it fails to present a full picture of the three cases it cited.

In the Daniel Taylor case, the defendant signed a highly detailed 25-page, court-reported confession in which he accurately described the building and the apartment where the murder took place, the method of the murder, where the two victims was placed on a sofa after she was shot. These facts corroborate the evidence from the murder scene. Taylor divulged these details within three hours of the arrest. The Salient facts are corroborated by his co-defendants, all of whom also named Taylor as a participant in the murders.

Even though the evidence in the case supports the conviction and the appellate court has upheld that conviction, we have continued to work with the defense attorney Kathleen Zellner whenever she has come to us with new thoughts or information.

In the case of Harold Hill and Dan Young Jr., they both confessed to a brutal murder and were subsequently convicted. These confessions were challenged, but both challenges were rejected and the confessions were admitted into evidence.

The editorial mentions that DNA from hairs and on a fingernail clipping from the murder scene did not match either Hill or Young. The fact that the DNA from the recovered hairs does not match either Hill or Young proves very little. There is no way to know the source of the substance found on the fingernail clipping.

The Michael Evans and Paul Terry case, however, is indeed troubling.

Recent DNA evidence shows that the semen recovered from the body of 9-year-old Lisa Cabassa does not match either man.

In the months since that discovery, prosecutors and investigators have spoken to the victim's parents, to police, to the original prosecutors and to the witnesses. This review continues in earnest while the two men are out on bond.

While these cases were brought long before I became state's attorney in 1996, it is my continuing obligation to see that justice is done and that any wrongs are made right. In two of the three cases the editorial cites, the evidence remains strong that those convicted are indeed guilty.

And to date, judges, juries and appellate courts have agreed.

Deon's Feedback

Devine's words about our case—Daniel Taylor's case—were both a painful reminder and a cold splash of reality. He described Taylor's detailed confession and the evidence that seemed to support the conviction. It was a narrative that, on the surface, seemed ironclad. He talked about Taylor's detailed account of the crime scene and how his co-defendants had corroborated his involvement. It was like watching a replay of a game you knew you'd lost, with each play reinforcing the crushing weight of our situation.

Yet, what really stung was the mention of the appellate court's decision and the ongoing work with Kathleen Zellner. Here was a case where the wheels of justice had seemingly moved on, leaving us to watch from the sidelines. It was like being told we were part of the show, only to be told later that our roles were insignificant. The hope that had risen with the early parts of the article seemed to deflate as quickly as it had appeared.

Then came the cases of Harold Hill and Dan Young Jr., whose confessions and subsequent convictions seemed to be upheld despite the DNA evidence not matching. The arguments about the DNA from the fingernail clippings not proving much felt like a dismissive pat on the back. It was as if they were telling us, "We've got this all figured out. Your concerns are just noise."

But the Michael Evans and Paul Terry case, with its recent DNA evidence that did not match either man, was where the article struck a different chord. For a moment, it felt like there was a glimmer of hope, a sign that the system was willing to reconsider and rectify its mistakes. Yet, this was tempered by the ongoing review and the knowledge that the two men were still out on bond. It felt like a partial victory that did little to alleviate the larger struggle faced by those still incarcerated.

The article was a reminder of the unpredictable nature of our fight. Each piece of news, each new development, was a potential turning point that could either lift us up or slam us back down. And while Devine's article offered some hope, it also reinforced the reality that our fight was far from over.

So, despite the emotional roller coaster that the Tribune's article took us on, we never gave up hope. We continued to push forward, fueled by the belief that one day, our voices would be heard, and justice would finally prevail. We kept our eyes on the prize, determined not to let the delays and setbacks deter us from our ultimate goal. The fight was long and arduous, but hope, once ignited, was a flame we refused to let extinguish.

Paul's Poem; "Read it and Weep" 2004

I don't understand the concept of human beings
related to the life that the society brings
About the world, or how we get involved in it,
uncharacteristically living, trying to uphold an image
thinking about warfare going on changes to welfare
Politics is a big topic, Social Security and childcare.
Don't get me wrong. I know this affect the sum,
but we talk about this every year, but still, nothing's done.
I want people to open their eyes and realize
it's bigger than saying, well, at least I tried
environmental hazards and no worldly solutions.
Where's the cure for AIDS? Why does the World increase pollution?
America has such a deficit, but we call it a crisis.
The Government Board is in debt, so all they want to do is raise
prices.

The Hazel Boyz

What are the real problems of this world and why do we sympathize with it?
Why do we stay with what we can relate to or identify with?
We look for recognition as some for notoriety. All to say, I was involved in this sadistic society.
War is going on in Iraq and in Syria, but the real war is going on in places like Nigeria,
Africa, Israel. Places follow all criteria, still infested and wasted, covered with bacteria.
Everybody gets the same opportunity and time,
but a certain environment can make you result in doing crime.
Don't get me wrong. We blame ourselves. School, get free courses,
but a single parent raising children is hard without resources,
doing crime is secondary, and sometimes lasts on peoples list,
but by any means necessary, is sometimes a survival kit
poverty, war and child abuses in newspapers and magazines.
Then they take away things that help us, and then try to raise gasoline.
Who does that effect? I say the poor and the needy. But then we still vote and elect for the rich and the greedy.
We put in office the same person we just got rid of.
The reason why it doesn't work is because here's another one the government sent us.
Why is the news bad news? Child abuse, murder, rapes and robberies,
or why do we celebrate tragedies and smile at other countries in poverty?
People say, okay, now, what are you going to do about it?
Should I talk about guns and drugs and why prisons are overcrowded?
People say, one voice makes a difference. Understanding things is still complicated.
How many people stood up and then died or got assassinated?
Why do a Democrat lose one race and then won't run again?
And if he does run, how come all of a sudden, he's a Republican?
They use trickery and deception to have us ride with the opposition
and come out with no inventions to draw our eyes off the real intention.
If we struggle, we go to agencies and bureaus,
And then we keep lying to our kids about life and fantasy heroes
finding old letters of crooked government backgrounds,

Still The Voiceless

And praise the Society for graduating in cap and gowns.
If we break the law, we get disciplined and punished.
Isn't that something?
The police and the government do it and they get nothing.
I'm tired of this world always separating criminals
like they only come in certain forms.
They also come political.

Chapter 19

A Lifeline From The Press

Deon's Thoughts

As I stared at the article from the Chicago Tribune, my heart raced with a mix of disbelief and cautious optimism. The headline read: "5 Inmates Ask Judge for Hearing in 1992 Double Murder," and beneath it, the article recounted our desperate plea for justice. This was the break we had all been waiting for.

For years, it felt like we were trapped in a nightmare, where no matter how much we pleaded or how many times we shouted our innocence, it fell on deaf ears. But now, there was a sliver of hope. Kathleen Zellner, our dedicated attorney, was pushing for a new hearing. We were finally getting back in front of a judge, with new evidence and a renewed sense of determination. It felt like this was all we needed—just one more chance to prove our innocence and show the world that we had absolutely nothing to do with that horrific crime.

CHICAGO TRIBUNE: *5 inmates ask judge for hearing in 1992 double murder*

By Maurice Possley and Steve Mills
February 11, 2004
The attorney for five men imprisoned for a double murder they insist

A Lifeline From The Press

they did not commit asked a Cook County circuit judge Tuesday for a hearing to present evidence that shows they are innocent.

The petition, filed by attorney Kathleen Zellener, contends that Chicago detectives coerced the men to falsely confess to the Nov. 16, 1992, murders of Jeffrey Lassiter and Sharon Haugabook in an apartment at 910 W. Agatite Ave., even though records show one of the men was in a police lockup at the time.

The Cook County state's attorney began investigating the convictions of Daniel Taylor and four other men after a Tribune article raised questions about whether they were wrongly convicted, even though police said all of them had confessed to taking part in the crime.

Convicted along with Taylor were Paul Phillips, Deon Patrick, Lewis Garder and Dennis Mixon. Taylor, Mixon and Patricki were sentenced to life in prison, and Phillips and Garner are serving 30-year terms.

All five, and three others, confessed and implicated each other. But arrest and bond records show Taylor had been under arrest in a police lockup and was not released until after the murders were committed. Charges against two of the three others were dropped or thrown out and the third was acquitted.

The petition cites police reports that show Taylor was locked up for disorderly conducts at 6:45 p.m. on the night of the murders. A bond slip showed he was not released from the Town Hall District lockup until 10 p.m. The murders, according to police, occurred at 8:43 p.m.

Jerry Lawrence, spokesman for Cook County State's Atty. Richard Devine, declined to comment because prosecutors had not seen the petition.

But in a letter to the Tribune last year, Devine noted that Taylor "signed a highly detailed 25-page, court-reported confession in which he accurately described the building and the apartment where the murder took place, the method of the murder, where the two victims were shot and how one of the victims was placed on a sofa after she was shot."

Devine said that the confession corroborated the evidence from the murder scene and that Taylor divulged the details within three hours of his arrest for the killings in December 1992. However, Devine said his office would continue to work with Zellner if she brought new information.

A Tribune investigation in December 2001 and a follow-up in

January 2003 uncovered new information–cited in the petition– that suggested the men were wrongly convicted.

Adrian Grimes, a drug dealer, testified at Taylor's trial that he saw Taylor on the street at 7:30 p.m. on the night of the murders, but Grimes told the \Tribune that he had lied at the request of detectives.

Documents never obtained by Taylor's defense lawyer, along with interviews, undermined a report by two police officers, filed weeks after authorities learned of Taylor's jail records, that said they saw him on the street at 9:30 that night.

Another witness, Willie Triplett, who had never before been interviewed by police, told the Tribune he was outside the apartment when the murders occurred and saw Mixon leave the building before shots were fired. Triplett said Taylor and the others were not involved.

Mixon, in an interview at Stateville Correctional Center, told the Tribune he went into the building with two other men to collect money from Lassiter and fled just before the shots were fired. He said that Taylor, Phillps and the other defendants were not involved and that he never even met them until he was arrested in the case.

Deon Continues

I could almost see the courtroom filled with the weight of anticipation. We were ready to tell our side of the story, to expose the truth buried under layers of false confessions and corrupted testimonies. The article revealed how the records showed that I had been locked up at the time of the murders. This was exactly the kind of evidence we needed to challenge the shaky foundations of our convictions.

Reading about the Tribune's investigation, I felt a surge of hope. It was like a lifeline had been thrown to us. The article mentioned the new information that cast serious doubts on our guilt. Adrian Grimes, who had testified against us, admitted to lying at the detectives' request. Willie Triplett's account of seeing Mixon leave the apartment before the shots were fired was a critical piece of evidence that supported our innocence. The more I read, the more I felt that maybe, just maybe, this was the turning point we had longed for.

But amid the growing excitement, there was a nagging sense of

A Lifeline From The Press

uncertainty. This was 2004, and despite the renewed efforts and fresh evidence, ten years had already passed since we were wrongfully convicted. The years had been cruel and relentless. The promise of a new hearing was a beacon of hope, but it was still just that—a promise. We had been let down before, and while the article fueled our optimism, it also reminded us of how much we had already endured.

As I absorbed the details, I couldn't help but feel a mix of hope and trepidation. The fight was far from over. This was another step in a long journey, and while it was a significant step, the path to freedom was still fraught with challenges. We had to stay strong, keep pushing, and hold on to the hope that this time, the truth would prevail.

We needed this chance to be heard, to present our evidence and clear our names. And as we prepared for this new chapter, I clung to the belief that justice would eventually come, even if it had taken far too long. The article was more than just a report; it was a glimmer of hope in the darkness, a signal that our fight was not in vain.

Paul's Poem: "Who's Changing" 2005

I'm really confused, trying to understand why the police aren't changing.
It's amazing and ashamed that
I have to look them in their face,
because if I let my head hang down,
it becomes a spiritual hanging.
My beast is what I'm taming to be released is what I crave.
The protection comes when it's you that needs to be saved,
but it's me that I'm saving.
My mission is to allow God to have my full submission,
because what I have bottled up in my body, I don't get three wishes.
So, listen to this sentence, and please pay attention
their intention to remove black kids from society was their mission.
We got convicted. They have no consequences or conviction.
I guess black kids are the real drugs in this neighborhood.
That's why the police have a real addiction.

Chapter 20

Counting Down The Days To Half-Time

Back in the early '90s, if you were sentenced to double digits in prison, you knew you'd only have to serve half that time. For Lewis and Paul, two of five of the co-defendants, that meant their 30-year sentences from 1992 were coming up on the 15-year mark by August 2007. Their release dates were finally in sight, just around the corner. While they were preparing for the possibility of freedom, the rest of them—those still tangled in the system with no set date—had to watch and wait, hoping that their time would come soon.

Lewis' Thoughts

The days leading up to my release were a whirlwind of emotions. After spending over a decade behind bars for a crime I didn't commit, I found myself both excited and terrified as my release date approached. I remember feeling nervous—really nervous—because even though I was finally getting out, the world had changed so much in my absence. I was stepping out into a life that had moved on without me, and that thought alone was enough to make my heart race.

I didn't know what to expect when I got out. How do you rebuild your life when everything you once knew has been stripped away? My mind was racing with questions, doubts, and fears. I was leaving a world I had adapted to for years, a world where I knew the rules—even if they were unjust. And now, I was going back into a world where I didn't know the rules anymore.

When I found out that I would be getting out early, a mix of emotions hit me like a freight train. Relief was there, of course. But there was also a deep, gnawing fear. What if I couldn't adjust? What if the world had moved on without me and I was left behind, unable to catch up? It was a sunny day on August 8, 2007, the day I was released, but it felt gloomy in my heart. The sun was shining, sure, but I couldn't shake the coldness inside me.

No one was there to pick me up. I had to catch a bus, and even that simple act felt strange. I was at the bus station, and it hit me that I wasn't really free—at least not in my mind. The habits of prison life were still with me. As I stood there, waiting for the bus, a guy near me was on his earpiece, and for a split second, I thought he was talking to me. I turned around, ready to confront him, but then I realized he wasn't even aware of my existence. It was a strange reminder that, even though I was out of prison, a part of me was still trapped there.

The bus ride was long, and when I finally got to Chicago, my step dad picked me up. I was supposed to parole to my sister's house, but things didn't go as planned. The paperwork got messed up, and when I arrived, my sister and her husband weren't really in the best place themselves. They were in and out of jail, and before long, I ended up having to take care of my niece and nephew, trying to piece together some semblance of a life.

But life on house arrest wasn't easy. The people I was staying with eventually got evicted, and I had nowhere to go. I felt like I was on a merry-go-round, constantly being spun in circles, unable to find my footing. At one point, I ended up back in jail, not because I did anything wrong, but because I had nowhere to go. My mom had moved back down south, leaving me stuck in Zion, feeling more lost and alone than ever.

I bounced around from place to place, staying with relatives who didn't really want me there. It wasn't until I met my wife that things started to turn around. We met through one of my cousins at a carwash, and from that moment on, we were inseparable. She helped me in ways I can't even begin to describe. Without her, I might have ended up back in prison or worse. She saved me from myself, from the darkness that was threatening to pull me under.

But it wasn't just my wife who helped me. My mother-in-law played a big role too. She helped me find jobs and get off parole, and for that, I'll always be grateful. My first job out was at the carwash where I met my wife. It wasn't much, but it was a start. I saved every penny I could, and eventually, we were able to get our own place. We were living with her mom at first, paying bills, and trying to build a life together.

The transition from prison to freedom wasn't easy. There were so many triggers—things that would set off that old prison mentality. Crowds made me anxious, and I found myself avoiding social situations whenever possible. I preferred to stay at home, behind closed doors, where I felt safe. The doors always had to be closed, though. I couldn't stand the feeling of being exposed, vulnerable.

There were other triggers too. Anytime I saw the police, my heart would race. Even though I had my license and was doing everything right, I couldn't shake the fear that they were coming for me, that somehow, they would find a reason to take me back to prison. It was a constant battle, trying to convince myself that I was really free.

Paul's Poem: "The Rock" 2007

No substance about life,
no foundation to land on.
Where's your facts of life?
We got proof. Y'all dead wrong.
We all were handpicked.
Y'all stand weak. We stand strong.
It's not because we are above y'all. We just had something to stand on
The cross we picked up. Is something that we held on to.
The only time y'all pick it up is to say, shame on you.
Well, we got opportunities, but y'all didn't give us the same ones too.
The only difference is y'all got lies to hang on.
We got the truth to hang on to.

My release date was August 31, 2007. When I first got released, it was like stepping into a world I had long forgotten. The first thing I remember is my dad picking me up from Robinson Correctional Center. My dad, he's always had this quirky sense of humor, always trying to lighten up the mood, but that day, it was different. He pulled me into this tight hug, and before I knew it, he was crying. I mean, this was a man who never showed a tear, not even when his own father died. So, to see him break down like that... it hit me hard. It was like the weight of all those years, all that lost time, just came crashing down on both of us.

After we processed out, I changed into the clothes he brought me, and we headed home to Wheeling, Illinois. I was on house arrest for the first three months, and it felt like I was still trapped in a way, like I had one foot still in prison. They put an ankle monitor on me, and that thing was a constant reminder that I wasn't truly free yet. But I tried to focus on getting back on my feet. I wanted to find a job, maybe go back to school, just do something to start over. But every time I applied somewhere, my past kept haunting me. Those old charges kept popping up, and employers just didn't want to take a chance on me.

I remember feeling this overwhelming sense of frustration. Here I was, out of prison, but I still couldn't move forward. At that time, a friend of mine, someone I knew before I got locked up, was struggling with cancer. I'd take her to her appointments, trying to help out where I could. Meanwhile, my dad was also battling cancer. It felt like I was surrounded by illness and loss. Then, I met Shanette Jefferson, and we started dating. Things seemed like they were looking up, but life had other plans. She got pregnant with twins, and just as I thought I'd have a new start, my dad passed away. A few months later, the twins died during childbirth. It was like life kept punching me in the gut, one tragedy after another.

Losing my dad, and then the twins, put me into a deep depression. I felt like I was drowning, with no way out. I tried to keep myself busy, applying for jobs, going to school, but nothing stuck. Every time I got close to something, my past would slam the door in my face. I ended up doing temp work, mostly in warehouses, but even there, it was like I couldn't catch a break. I'd work for 80 days, just shy of when they had to hire me full-time, and then they'd fire me, only to call me back a month later to start the cycle all over again.

After a few rounds of that, I decided I couldn't keep doing it. I needed to find something else, something that would give me some stability. I ended up working security at a nursing home, just trying to make ends meet. But even then, it was tough. My record kept coming up, making it hard to even get that job. Eventually, I went back to school to get my degree in computers, thinking maybe that would give me a fresh start. I had learned a lot in prison, took every class I could, got certified in computer technology, but when I got out, it didn't seem to matter. My past was always there, like a shadow I couldn't escape.

One night, I was out, just trying to forget everything, when something changed. I don't know if it was the sunrise or just exhaustion, but I felt like God was telling me I couldn't keep living like that. That's when I decided I needed to clear my name, to finally put all this behind me for good. I started reaching out to lawyers, but most of them said my case was too risky, too complicated. It felt like I was hitting the same wall over and over again.

Chapter 21

When Hope Got Tricky

Daniel's Thoughts

Around the time when I started working in X house, things were changing. I was transitioning with my legal team and exploring new avenues for my case. I had just received a letter from Kathleen Zellner, wishing me good luck on my quest for freedom. It was a boost, a glimmer of hope, especially since I was also in discussions with Northwestern University's Center on Wrongful Convictions about taking my case pro bono. It felt like a pivotal moment—a chance for a new chapter in my fight for justice.

Then, the article hit. The Chicago Tribune article titled "Where Was Daniel Taylor?" was published on September 4, 2007. I remember reading it and feeling a rush of emotions—anger, frustration, and profound hurt. The article highlighted the flaws in my case, the inconsistencies, and the damning details of my confession, which I had always claimed was coerced.

CHICAGO TRIBUNE: *Where was Daniel Taylor?*
September 4, 2007

The scrutiny of death penalty cases has slowed since former Gov. George Ryan cleared out Death Row. Most of the obvious cases of wrongful *conviction that could be proved with DNA testing have been proved. A handful of inmates have started repopulating Death Row under new convictions and sentences. What remains are lower-profile cases where people serving long sentences may not belong in prison.*

Daniel Taylor is one of those cases. He's serving his 14th year of a life sentence for a double murder.

Taylor doesn't have DNA evidence to prove he didn't commit the crime. The vast majority of crimes don't involve DNA evidence. But Taylor does have police records that show he was in jail when Jeffrey Lassiter and Sharon Haugabook were killed in their Uptown apartment in 1992.

Taylor was 17 when he was picked up by police two weeks after the murders of Lassiter and Haugabook. Taylor claims police hit him with a flashlight. He says they told him they'd let him go as soon as he confessed. So he did, in a 25-page statement. He later stated that police gave him details about the crime and let him read another suspect's confession, which helped him fill out details for his own confession.

Shortly after he confessed, Taylor recalled that he had been in a police district lockup on a disorderly conduct charge when the murder was said to have occurred. Several law-enforcement officers responsible for arresting, transporting, booking, receiving, approving charges and signing a bond slip corroborated Taylor's claim that he was in custody at the time.

Faye McCoy, who lived in the building where the murders took place, said she got a good look at people who walked out of the victims' apartment just after the crime ... and said Taylor wasn't one of them.

She told the Tribune that prosecutors tried to get her to link Taylor to the crime, in part by showing her his confession. "And I wouldn't cooperate. I wouldn't lie. They said it's not lying because it's in the confessions," McCoy said.

Records from the lockup weren't enough to convince a jury, though. At trial, prosecutors argued that people don't con-fess to crimes they do not commit. "Paperwork is not foolproof," one prosecutor said. "But I'll tell you what is fool-proof. And what is foolproof are the defendant's own words."

But they're not foolproof. Illinois has had several cases in which people falsely confessed to serious offenses. Young people and people with low intelligence are particularly vulnerable to suggestion by investigators. Those who have been tortured or held in a room for hours on end sometimes say whatever is necessary to make the interrogation stop. The chance of a false or coerced confession is one of the main reasons that state law now requires police to record police interrogations in homicide cases in Illinois.

Prosecutors still believe Taylor is guilty. "We never thought this was a false confession," said John Gorman, a spokes-man for Cook County State's Atty. Richard Devine. "We thought this was a confession so replete with detail and given so soon after the arrest, our position hasn't changed."

It should.

Eight people were arrested for the murders. Their various statements implicated each other. But one man who admitted that he did commit the murder, Dennis Mixon, told the Tribune he never met any of the others charged until he arrived in prison. Mixon said another man committed the murders with him; that man has never been charged.

Taylor and four others were convicted. One has been released from prison and another is scheduled to be released Mon-day. Daniel Taylor's hopes for new consideration of his case rest with Circuit Judge Bertina Lampkin, who may agree later this month to hold a hearing.

There are too many questions to let this case die while Daniel Taylor sits in prison.

Daniel Continues

It was infuriating to see my situation laid out so plainly, yet still so misunderstood by the public and the legal system. George Lemkin's denial of my appeal had left me once again in the position of fighting this battle alone. The rejection was a punch to the gut, especially after putting everything I had into proving my innocence. It felt like every time I took a step forward, I was being pushed two steps back.

Despite the setback, my hope was far from extinguished. I was still in discussions with Northwestern University and was meeting with Karen Daniel and Judith Royal from the Center on Wrongful Convictions twice a month. The process was slow, but each meeting was a step closer to having them officially represent me. We meticulously reviewed the case, examined the evidence, and discussed strategies for filing a petition for actual innocence.

When Hope Got Tricky

Emotionally, I was a whirlwind. The denial by Judge Lampkin was a heavy blow, but talking to Karen Daniel and the team provided a sense of relief, even if it was fleeting. It was reassuring to know that they were on my side, even if the legal battles were ongoing and the future remained uncertain. Mentally, I was in a more stable place than I had been in the past, but the weight of self-representation and the fear of not doing things correctly were constant companions.

While all this was happening, I had a job in prison—cell house help. It was a fancy way of saying janitor. My duties included passing out food, sweeping, mopping, and waxing floors. It was the only way I could earn some money, which was essential since financial support from the outside was minimal. I made $45 a month, but it was a lifeline, both financially and mentally. Deon's support was crucial during these times, providing me with necessary items and emotional encouragement.

Despite the challenges, I focused on staying stable and keeping my spirits intact. My daily routine, my interactions with Deon, and my ongoing meetings with Karen and Judith were my anchors. I was fighting for my innocence, not just for myself but for my co-defendants who also didn't commit the crime. The battle was far from over, but every step, every conversation, and every piece of evidence brought me closer to the truth and, hopefully, to the justice I had long been seeking.

Deon's Thoughts

It's funny how time can stretch and compress depending on what you're waiting for. Four years and five months—that's how long it had been since the Chicago Tribune last wrote about our case on June 23, 2003. It was like someone had finally opened a window in a suffocating room, letting in a breath of fresh air. We had momentum back then. We were hopeful, determined, and we felt like the truth was on the verge of coming to light. But then, time started playing tricks on us. Days turned into months, and months into years. The momentum we had felt so strongly began to wane. It was like being on a roller coaster that had slowly creaked its way to the top, only to get stuck there, suspended in mid-air. The anticipation was excruciating. Every day we waited for something, anything, to push us forward, but nothing came.

Hope is a tricky thing. You try to hold onto it, but after a while, it becomes heavy, almost like a burden. You start to question whether it's worth carrying around anymore. We were all feeling it—the slow, grinding weight of uncertainty. The articles, the attention, the brief moments of public interest—they had all faded away, leaving us alone with our thoughts and our doubts.

Then, on September 4, 2007, everything changed.

I remember the day like it was yesterday. The buzz in the air was different, almost electric. I got word that there was a new article in the Tribune, something about Daniel, something that might bring the truth back into the spotlight. When I finally got my hands on it, my heart was pounding so hard I could barely focus. But as I read the headline —"Where was Daniel Taylor?"—I felt something shift inside me.

It was as if someone had flipped a switch. That roller coaster we'd been stuck on for so long suddenly jerked back to life, pulling us upward once again. The article reignited everything we had felt four years earlier —the hope, the determination, the belief that the end was in sight.

But this time, it felt different. It felt like we were on the verge of something real, something tangible. The story wasn't just about revisiting the past; it was about shining a light on the truth that had been buried for too long. It was about asking the questions that had never been fully answered, demanding accountability from those who had tried to silence us. For the first time in years, I felt that maybe, just maybe, we were nearing the outcome we deserved. It was like a beacon in the darkness, guiding us forward. And for the first time in a long time, I allowed myself to believe that this nightmare might actually have an end—that justice might finally be within our reach. We were back on that roller coaster, but this time, we weren't going down. We were on our way up, and this time, I knew we were heading toward the light at the end of the tunnel.

Chapter 22

A Year Of Transition In Stark Darkness

Daniel's Thoughts

In 2012, I found myself navigating the harsh confines of Menard Correctional Center, a supermax facility in Menard, Illinois. This was a significant transition from Stateville Correctional Center, where I had been held since September 8, 2008. Menard, situated in Southern Illinois near the Missouri River, was known for its harsh conditions and, unfortunately, its deep-seated racial tensions. For many, the transition to Menard was daunting; for me, it was an opportunity to reshape my approach to the challenges I faced.

When I first arrived at Menard, the adjustment was overwhelming. The facility was known not only for its high-security measures but also for its unforgiving environment. The stark reality of prison life hit hard: the basic necessities of life were often out of reach. Simple things like soap, deodorant, toothpaste, and even food snacks were not easily obtainable. The meals provided were often subpar, adding to the everyday struggles. The financial help I had hoped for from the outside world was non-existent, leaving me to fend for myself in a place where survival meant making every resource count.

As the months wore on, my focus shifted to finding ways to improve my situation. With no external financial support, I needed to find a job within the prison system. A job would not only alleviate some of the financial pressures but also provide a sense of purpose and routine. The thought of earning even a small amount of money to buy essential items was a beacon of hope amidst the daily grind of incarceration.

2012 was not just a year of adjustment; it was a year of strategic planning and personal growth. I immersed myself in understanding the legal intricacies of my case, hoping to find a pathway to justice. This year marked a pivotal moment in my legal journey. I dedicated countless hours to meeting with legal experts, including Karen Daniel and Judith Royal, to discuss my case. Our discussions were thorough, focusing on the legal strategies necessary to prove my innocence and address the wrongful accusations against me.

During these meetings, we worked tirelessly on crafting a petition that would serve as a critical component in my fight for justice. The aim was clear: to prove my innocence and challenge the evidence used against me. The process was painstakingly detailed, requiring a deep dive into legal documents, case files, and a strategic plan to counter the accusations.

The environment at Menard, while harsh, was the backdrop against which I was refining my resilience and resourcefulness. Each day presented new challenges, but it also provided opportunities for growth. I was learning to adapt to the realities of life in a supermax prison while simultaneously working towards a brighter future.

The transition year of 2012 was marked by a dual focus on personal adaptation and legal advocacy. While the conditions were far from ideal, it was in this crucible of adversity that I found new strengths and determination. My efforts to secure a job within the prison system and my relentless pursuit of legal redress were the cornerstones of my strategy to reclaim my life and prove my innocence.

As the year progressed, I remained hopeful. The challenges of 2012, while significant, were also a testament to my resilience and commitment to justice. It was a year of laying the groundwork for future success, with each step taken in the harsh reality of Menard Correctional Center contributing to the broader goal of achieving justice and freedom.

CHICAGO TRIBUNE: 'Strong proof' he's innocent\ More documents indicate that inmate was in a police lockup when 1992 double murder occurred

April 2, 2012

By Steve Mills

The Illinois attorney general's office has opened an in-depth examination of how Cook County prosecutors have handled the trial and nearly two decades of appeals in a controversial 1992 double murder case that sent a teenager to prison for life, even though records showed he was in a Chicago police lockup when the crime occurred, according to court documents and interviews.

At issue is whether prosecutors failed to turn over key information to defense lawyers that would have helped the case of Daniel Taylor, whose defense at trial seemed ironclad: that he had been arrested on unrelated charges before the murders occurred and was not released until after.

Taylor's case, in turn, casts doubt on the entire criminal investigation, since eight suspects in all confessed and impli-cated each other.

A three-judge panel of the 7th U.S. Circuit Court of Appeals that included Judge Richard Posner recently found Taylor's claims were worth pursuing and took the unusual step of granting his request to file a second appeal in federal court -- a move that could lead to a new trial. And that was before the attorney general's office began digging deep into the case and uncovered additional documents it said were not turned over to Taylor.

"When combined with the testimony of (a) newly revealed witness and the newly disclosed police reports," the judges wrote in an order late last year, "this is strong proof that Taylor's participation in the crime was physically impossible. In contrast, the circumstances surrounding the non-videotaped confession are suspect."

The case against Taylor and the seven other defendants was the focus of the Tribune's 2001 investigation "Cops and Confessions." Five of the eight defendants were convicted and sent to prison, and Taylor was sentenced to life without possibility of parole. The Tribune has continued to *investigate the case. Among the subsequent revelations: A Taylor co-defendant said he and several other men committed the murders and that Taylor and the others who were arrested are innocent.*

In some cases, crucial documents or witnesses that can turn a prosecution upside down do not surface for years. That it is happening in a case that has received such scrutiny may raise questions about who in the prosecutors' office had knowledge of the documents and why they were allegedly withheld.

The failure to turn over material that can help a defendant's case at trial is among the most serious violations a prosecu-tor can commit.

The current inquiry began as the attorney general's office took over the federal appeal from Cook County prosecutors, a routine job for litigators in the office of Attorney General Lisa Madigan.

As lawyers dug deeper into the case and began to review the state's attorney's files, they found additional documents that, under the law, they believed should have been turned over to Taylor's trial attorney but had been withheld, accord-ing to filings in federal court and correspondence between the attorney general's office and Taylor's current attorney.

Those documents would have bolstered Taylor's defense at trial, the court filings say.

"It's simply unacceptable that this evidence has remained hidden for 19 years," said Karen Daniel, an attorney at the Center on Wrongful Convictions at Northwestern University law school and Taylor's lawyer. "The correct thing for the state's attorney to do now is to go into court immediately and have the conviction set aside. ... Daniel has been locked up for more than half his life, for a crime he didn't even commit and without the benefit of a fair trial. Any further delay only magnifies the injustice."

Dan Kirk, chief of staff for Cook County State's Attorney Anita Alvarez, said prosecutors were cooperating with the attorney general's office. He said they were studying the case file as quickly as possible to determine if prosecutors had an obligation to turn over the documents and whether they were withheld.

"We don't know at this point whether they were turned over or not. But we're going to find out," said Kirk, who described the effort as a challenge

because of the age of the case. "I don't feel comfortable taking anybody's word for it until we ourselves do an exhaustive review."

Sally Daly, Alvarez's spokeswoman, put a finer point on the issue, saying the office considers the claim "an unsubstan-tiated allegation."

"We're working with the attorney general," Daly said. "We're also reviewing the entire case file, to analyze the matter and to review the notes that have been raised in the context of the totality of the entire case. We're trying to do this as quickly as possible."

Taylor was 17 and living mostly on the streets when he and the others were charged with the November 1992 shooting deaths of Sharon Hauga-book and Jeffrey Lassiter. According to the confessions, the shootings stemmed from a dispute between Lassiter and one of the suspects, Dennis Mixon. Mixon later admitted he and at least two other men, one of them now in prison for another murder, committed the crime.

Taylor was questioned by police about two weeks after the murders. But after police obtained a statement from him, Taylor remembered he had been locked up on the night of the arrests, and he told detectives. They then began to investigate his claim and found records that showed Taylor was, in fact, behind bars. Police then said they found evidence that undercut that claim and supported Taylor's confession.

At trial, prosecutors told jurors that Taylor's confession tied him to the crime; indeed, all eight suspects implicated all the others in their confes-sions. Seven of the eight -- all except for Mixon -- have maintained their innocence. Prosecu-tors at trial were Thomas Needham -- who became a top aide to former Mayor Richard Daley, then a top Police Department lawyer and now is in private practice -- and Jeanne Bischoff, who is still in the prosecutors' office.

Needham and Bischoff could not be reached for comment.

Taylor's lawyer, Nathan Diamond-Falk, showed jurors an enlarged arrest report and bond slip showing Taylor was ar-rested two hours before the 8:45 p.m. murders, taken to the now-shuttered Town Hall police station at Halsted and Addison streets, and was not released until 10 p.m.

Police officers from the station testified in Taylor's defense, but the testimony was less than robust in part because Tay-lor's lawyer did not have all of the documents generated in the case. Prosecutors undermined the officers' testimony, too, suggesting they were covering up for breaking police rules by releasing Taylor early.

The issue of what prosecutors turned over to the defense has been simmering in the case for some time. In the Tribune's investigation, documents were found that were not turned over to Taylor's trial attorney. Those showed police were try-ing to find a man who shared a lockup cell with Taylor. That man told the Tribune that once police found him and he said he remembered being locked up with a young black man, the police lost interest in him and never contacted him again. Had Taylor's trial lawyer had the reports, he could have called the man as a witness to try to bolster the alibi that he was behind bars.

That was the issue the federal appeals court recently ruled on and said bolstered Taylor's claim he could not have com-mitted the crime.

The new documents are handwritten notes of interviews of the officers working at the station the night Taylor was ar-rested. They were prepared by David Styler, a prosecutor who now works for Aon Corp., who made the grand jury presentation in Taylor's case. In the notes, several of the officers are certain Taylor was in the lockup when Taylor and the records say he was. One officer, James Gillespie, is quoted saying "he's convinced" that Taylor was there at 10 p.m., words that are stronger than his trial testi-mony. A sergeant is quoted saying Taylor was in the lockup when he left work at 9 p.m.

Styler and Gillespie could not be reached for comment.

Other officers working in the station that evening, according to the notes, also provided information that supported Tay-lor's alibi.

In court filings and correspondence, the attorney general's office says these notes should have been given to Diamond-Falk before trial but it believes they were not. The office says the notes are important because they "arguably memorial-ize potentially exculpatory conversations with police officers tending to corroborate (Taylor's) alibi defense."

Officials at the attorney general's office declined to comment.

Those notes go to the heart of Taylor's defense and would have allowed Diamond-Falk to question the police officers more effectively as well as fend off prosecutors' attempts to undermine Taylor's alibi. It is the second time documents have surfaced that likely hindered Diamond-Falk's *ability to defend Taylor, who is being held at Menard Correctional Center.*

Diamond-Falk declined to comment, saying he was likely to become a witness as Taylor's appeals continue in federal court.

"The statements of the police officers supported (Taylor's) defense. They did not support the prosecutors' suggestion at trial that the police lockup records were falsified or inaccurate," said Daniel, Taylor's attorney. "Prosecutors are required by law to disclose this type of evidence."

Taylor's case now is in both federal and state court, and he said he remains hopeful he can finally prove his innocence and win his freedom.

Deon's Thoughts

It's been five long years since the last article in the Chicago Tribune. Five years of uncertainty, of waiting in silence, and wondering if the world had forgotten us. On April 2, 2012, that silence was shattered by a headline that reignited a flicker of hope in my heart: "Strong Proof He's Innocent: More Documents Indicate That Inmate Was in a Police Lockup When 1992 Double Murder Occurred."

When I first saw those words, it felt like time stood still. Nineteen years in—nineteen years of my life lost to a system that was supposed to protect the innocent, but instead, locked me away for a crime I didn't commit. The weight of those years pressed down on me as I read the article, my hands trembling, my breath caught in my throat. For the first time in a long while, I felt something stir inside me—something that had been buried beneath layers of despair and resignation: hope.

The article laid out evidence that had been hidden from us, evidence that had the power to change everything. It wasn't just any piece of evidence, but crucial documents proving that Daniel was in police lockup at the time of the murders. For years, we had screamed into the void, insisting on my innocence, but my voice was drowned out by the overwhelming force of the system. Now, here it was, in black and white, undeniable proof that we had been telling the truth all along.

As I read on, the words blurred together as tears filled my eyes. This was more than just an article; it was a lifeline. It confirmed what I had feared all along—that they had hidden evidence that could have exonerated us from the very beginning. This was a Brady violation, a breach of the law that required them to turn over all evidence, whether it helped or hindered us. But they chose to hide it. They chose to keep this evidence from us, from our lawyers, and from the court. They denied us the chance to prove our innocence.

And now, nineteen years later, that evidence had finally come to light. A higher court had found it, exposed their deceit, and passed it on to our lawyers. For the first time in nearly two decades, I felt a surge of hope. The walls that had confined me for so long seemed a little less suffocating, the bars a little less solid. There was a light at the end of this tunnel, faint but growing stronger with every word I read.

I felt a mix of emotions—anger at the injustice, sorrow for the years lost, and a cautious optimism that maybe, just maybe, this nightmare was coming to an end. But I also knew better than to get too carried away. The system had failed us before, and there were no guarantees. Yet, I couldn't help but feel that the tide was turning, that the truth was finally breaking through the cracks in the wall they had built around me.

This article was more than just news; it was a symbol of hope, of resilience, and of the fight that still lay ahead. I wasn't out of the woods yet, but for the first time in a long while, I felt like I was on the right path. The evidence was in our hands now, and with it, the power to rewrite the story that had been written for me nineteen years ago.

As I sat there, holding the paper in my hands, I made a silent promise to myself. I would not let these years define me. I would fight until the truth set me free. This article was just the beginning, the first crack in the wall. And I would do everything in my power to tear that wall down, brick by brick, until I could finally walk free.

Daniel's Feedback

Reading the Chicago Tribune article titled "Strong Proof He's Innocent: More Documents Indicate That Inmate Was in a Police Lockup When 1992 Double Murder Occurred," published on April 2, 2012, was a moment filled with a tumult of emotions for me. As I absorbed the words on the page, there was no sense of surprise; I had long known

A Year Of Transition In Stark Darkness

that evidence existed to exonerate me. It wasn't the revelation that shocked me—it was the resurgence of feelings I had worked so hard to overcome.

I felt a familiar wave of hurt and disbelief wash over me, emotions that had once taken me to the brink of despair. Seeing the evidence I'd always believed in finally come to light was a mixed blessing. It brought a sense of validation, a relief that the State's Attorneys were stepping forward to present the evidence that had been buried for decades. It was like someone had finally taken a boulder off my shoulders—one that had weighed down on me for what felt like an eternity. But despite this relief, it also stirred a deep, visceral anger towards the system that had wronged me for so long.

The article was a stark reminder of the system's failures. My case was just one among many where wrongful convictions had led to deep personal suffering, and even death. While my story was painful, I couldn't ignore the darker reality of those who had lost their lives, executed for crimes they did not commit. The thought of innocent lives being snuffed out by a flawed system was a chilling reminder of just how broken the system could be.

The vindication I felt was tainted by the harsh reality of the prison system. My time behind bars had transformed me in ways I never anticipated. The stark contrast between being an innocent man surrounded by real criminals was a daily torment. I was forced to adopt a hardened demeanor, a survival mechanism in an environment where empathy and logic seemed like foreign concepts. The prison life, with its brutal illogic, had stripped me of a sense of normalcy and humanity.

By year 15, I found myself attempting to shut out the world beyond the prison walls. I had to focus on surviving within the confines of a system designed to break you. Forgetting about family, friends, and the outside world was a coping mechanism, not for peace, but for some semblance of survival. The struggle to maintain a shred of dignity and hope amidst the daily horrors of incarceration was a constant battle.

Reading the article was like a harsh spotlight on my own suffering, a reminder of how far I had come and how much further I still had to go. It was a fleeting glimmer of hope amid the darkness—a recognition of my suffering but also a testament to my unyielding fight for justice.

While the road ahead was still fraught with challenges, knowing that the truth was finally being acknowledged gave me a renewed, if cautious, sense of determination.

In the end, the article was not just about the evidence of my innocence; it was a stark reminder of the systemic failures and the cost of wrongful convictions. It reinforced my resolve to continue fighting, not just for myself, but for all those who had been wrongfully condemned. It was a bitter pill, but one that fueled my relentless pursuit of justice.

Chapter 23

The State's Reluctance To Acknowledge Truth

Daniel's Thoughts

May 7, 2012, was a day I had been waiting for with a mix of trepidation and cautious hope. The Chicago Tribune had just published an article titled "Was Alibi Ignored in Double Murder? New Evidence Raises Questions About '92 Slayings" by Steve Mills. As I read through the words, each sentence felt like a punch to the gut and a spark of light all at once.

I remember the intensity of that period vividly. We were entrenched in a battle that felt endless, fighting against a system that seemed determined to ignore the very evidence that could prove our innocence. Every day was a grind—trying to move forward while the walls felt like they were closing in. We were presenting evidence, making moves, and all the while, it felt like the authorities were more interested in digging their heels in than in considering the truth we were laying out before them.

The article was a double-edged sword. On one hand, it was incredibly validating to see that there was a growing recognition of the inconsistencies and flaws in the case against us. The Tribune's investigation was a beacon of truth in a fog of denial and bureaucratic resistance. But on the other hand, the battle was far from over. We were still in the thick of it, struggling to get our voices heard and our evidence acknowledged.

CHICAGO TRIBUNE: *Was alibi ignored in double murder? New evidence raises ques-tions about '92 slayings*

May 7, 2012

By Steve Mills

In 2002, Cook County prosecutors undertook what then was a most unusual inquiry: the reinvestigation of a double-murder case that sent five young men to prison, even though one of them had records showing he was in a Chicago po-lice lockup when the crime occurred.

About a year later, in March 2003, the office of then-State's Attorney Richard Devine announced that it was satisfied the convictions were sound in spite of a Tribune investigation that had uncovered new evidence suggesting that the young man, Daniel Taylor, was innocent.

Nearly a decade later, reports from that investigation -- obtained by the Tribune from sources after State's Attorney Anita Alvarez's office refused to make them available to the newspaper -- raise questions about how the investigation was done and whether it was even handed.

According to the reports, investigators and on some occasions prosecu-tors working under Devine interviewed the five men who were convicted and three other men who were arrested, some of them twice and one of them three times, plus some civilian witnesses linked to the case.

But investigators interviewed only one of the officers involved in the original investigation -- and, according to the reports, none of the officers who provided Taylor with his seemingly ironclad alibi. The investigators also did not ques-tion the detectives or prosecutors involved in taking the disputed confessions, according to the reports.

What's more, prosecutors announced they were certain Taylor was guilty after they had completed fewer than two-thirds of the interviews they ultimately conducted and before they spoke with Taylor or with a man identified as the real killer by the one defendant who admits he was at the crime scene.

The nearly 100 pages of reports suggest that Devine's office put effort into finding evidence to support the conviction but little into investigating Taylor's claim of innocence. The state's attorney's investigators sought out girlfriends of sev-eral of the suspects, an indication they were seeking *incriminating evidence. They also obtained pages and pages of CTA bus schedules; one former state's attorney's investigator who worked on the case said he had tried to determine if Taylor could have ridden a bus to the scene of the crime.*

In spite of all that, the suspects continued to assert their innocence. No one implicates Taylor, who is serving a sentence of life without parole, or any of the suspects save the one who admitted a role in the double murders, Dennis Mixon.

"I just don't see how the state's attorney's office can truly say they rein-vestigated Daniel's case, or reached any conclu-sions about his guilt or innocence, without going back and interviewing the police lockup officers who had him in cus-tody at the time of the murder," said Karen Daniel, who is Taylor's lawyer and an attorney at Northwestern University's Center on Wrongful Convictions. "They didn't do that. The ironic thing is that despite avoiding some of the most impor-tant witnesses, their reinves-tigation failed to turn up any evidence of Daniel's guilt and in fact provided additional sup-port of his innocence."

Alvarez's office, which did not handle the investigation but now is defending the conviction in state court -- Alvarez succeeded Devine -- declined to comment on the Taylor reinvestigation. The Illinois attorney general's office is han-dling the appeal as it moves through federal court.

Devine, who now is in private practice, did not review the reports from the reinvestigation but said he spoke with one person currently in the state's attorney's office and one person who used to be in the office to refresh his recollection of the case. He said he "can't imagine" that prosecu-tors and investigators did not interview the officers who supported Tay-lor's alibi -- although no reports indicate that such interviews were conducted. One of the investigators who worked on the reinvestigation, Ron Armata, said they would have documented any interview they conducted.

Devine said he never would have ordered an investigation that was not meant to be fair to Taylor or the other men convicted.

"This was meant to be a full investigation, and it's not my sense that anyone was playing games with it," said Devine, who added that the inves-tigators also followed any leads provided by Taylor's attorney at the time, Kathleen Zellner. "There was never any ambition to circumvent this."

Zellner said she provided leads to the prosecutors but also expected that they would investigate Taylor's alibi as part of their inquiry.

"Of course, I thought they would look at everything," she said.

Taylor, then 17, and seven other young men were arrested and charged with murder in the November 1992 shooting deaths of Sharon Haugabook and Jeffrey Lassiter in an apartment near Clarendon Park on Chicago's North Side.

According to police and prosecutors, four of the suspects went into the apartment and took part in the slayings while the other four stood outside as lookouts. All eight, police said, confessed and implicated each other.

After he was charged, Taylor remembered that he had been arrested the night of the slayings. And, in fact, police reports and records at the now-shuttered Town Hall police precinct showed Taylor was arrested for disorderly conduct about two hours before the 8:45 p.m. slayings and not released until close to 10 p.m.

The Tribune investigated the case as part of its December 2001 series "Cops and Confessions" and uncovered additional evidence of Taylor's innocence. That prompted Devine to launch the reinvestigation of the case, which he had said would be a fair search for evidence.

Since then, the Taylor case has continued to work its way through the criminal justice system. Most recently, it drew notice from the 7th U.S. Circuit Court of Appeals, which noted Taylor's powerful claim of innocence and questioned his confession in granting him an unusual new hearing.

As the Tribune reported in early April, the Illinois attorney general's office also has opened an in-depth examination of the Taylor case. In refusing to release the reports after the Tribune filed a Freedom of Information Act request, Alva-rez's office cited the attorney general's review. According to the reports, the investigation was supervised by prosecutors Alison Perona and Donald Lyman. Of 39 total interviews, 15 -- or more than one-third of them -- were conducted after prosecutors announced they were confident Taylor was guilty.

Perona, who is no longer a prosecutor, declined to comment. Lyman, who is still a prosecutor, also declined to com-ment.

The reinvestigation did not examine Taylor's alibi in spite of the fact that documents the attorney general's office believes were not turned over to the defense before Taylor's trial were in the prosecution's file and could have provided additional avenues of investigation.

That suggests prosecutors put more stock in Taylor's confession than the records and witnesses indicating he was in the lockup.

Devine said investigators from the state's attorney's office found nothing "against the weight of the evidence" that had convicted Taylor. What's more, he said prosecutors agreed to an evidentiary hearing, which Taylor lost, and that Tay-lor's case has been in court repeatedly.

"This thing has not been a behind-the-scenes deal," Devine said. "This has been before the courts on any number of oc-casions."

Daniel said it is clear to her that prosecutors had their minds made up before they launched the reinvestigation and did not make a good-faith effort to find evidence of Taylor's innocence. That, she said, was because they were wedded to his confession.

"This seems to be a case of confession tunnel vision," Daniel said. "They can't get beyond the fact that Daniel and some of his young friends confessed. ... In Daniel's case, the police records, the eyewitness accounts and newly disclosed in-formation from the state's attorney's own files prove that the confessions were false."

Daniel's Feedback

When that article came out, I was still caught in the mental grind of realizing that the state wasn't giving an inch. It was like they were fighting us tooth and nail every step of the way. The prosecutors weren't relinquishing, and they weren't acknowledging any of the evidence we'd put forth. Evidence that, to me and everyone who supported my fight, screamed my innocence.

I remember thinking, "How can they not see it?" The article brought to light so many questions about how the investigation was handled. It raised doubts about whether they had even attempted to be fair. They never interviewed the officers who could confirm my alibi, never spoke to those who could prove I was in a police lockup when the murders happened. And yet, they were convinced I was guilty. But what about the records? What about the witnesses? What about the cold, hard facts that said, "This guy couldn't have done it"? It was all there, plain as day, and yet they acted like it didn't exist. At that moment, I was reminded of just how stacked the deck was against me. I wasn't just fighting for myself—I was fighting for all of us. Every move I made towards proving my innocence, it wasn't just about me. It was about my co-defendants too. They were dragged into this mess just like I was, and every piece of evidence I presented was as much for them as it was for me. We were all in this together, bound by the injustice of a system that seemed determined to keep us down.

Reading that article, I felt like I was in the middle of a dogfight. I was grappling with everything I had, gathering all the evidence, all the documents, everything that could help me build a solid case for our innocence. Every detail, every scrap of evidence felt crucial, because we knew that once we filed our petition in court, we needed it to be airtight. But no matter how much we gathered, how strong our case became, it felt like they weren't going to let go. They weren't going to acknowledge anything that even hinted at my innocence. It was like they had tunnel vision, only seeing what they wanted to see, clinging to those false confessions like they were gospel.

In that moment, I felt an overwhelming sense of frustration and determination. I knew we had to keep pushing, keep fighting, because no one else was going to do it for us. It was up to us to make them see the truth. But I wasn't going to give up. I couldn't. For my co-defendants, for myself, and for everyone who believed in us, I had to keep going. We had to keep going. And that's exactly what we did.

Chapter 24

The Confession That Changed Everything

Deon's Thoughts

Here we are again, 10 days later, and the momentum is finally building. The article is out, and it's starting to feel like the world is paying attention to what's been going on all these years. I keep telling myself, "This is it, this is when things finally start to turn." The pressure is on, and we're staying on the gas, refusing to let up. It's like we've got the system in a corner now, and they can't ignore us anymore. They have to make a decision.

CHICAGO TRIBUNE: 19 years later, 'strong proof' of innocence
May 17, 2012

A decade ago, Cook County prosecutors took a long second look at the case against Daniel Taylor, who'd been sentenced to life in prison without parole for a 1992 double murder. Their review assured them they'd gotten it right the first time.

We disagreed then. We disagree now. And the evidence is still mounting.

Late last year, a federal appellate court granted Taylor permission to file a new appeal, which could lead to another trial. Since that ruling, more documents have surfaced that could have helped Taylor fight the charges in his 1995 trial.

Cook County's rare reinvestigation was prompted by the Tribune's 2001 "Cops and Confessions" series, which raised questions about the circumstances surrounding Taylor's confession and offered evidence to support the alibi that prose-cutors had shot down at trial: Taylor was in a police lockup when the murders took place.

The 7th U.S. Circuit Court of Appeals found that evidence compelling. The court said the evidence produced at trial, combined with "testimony of a newly revealed witness and the newly disclosed police reports" is "strong proof" that Taylor couldn't have participated in the crime. His confession, the judges wrote, was "suspect."

The evidence on which that decision was based wasn't new. It was available before the trial, but prosecutors didn't share it with Taylor's attorneys.

The Illinois attorney general's office, which is handling the case in federal court, has since discovered more documents that apparently weren't turned over, either. That evidence, too, could have bolstered Taylor's story.

Taylor was 17 at the time of the murders. There were no fingerprints or DNA to link him to the crime scene. No weapon was recovered. But jurors couldn't reconcile the teenager's alibi against the 25-page confession he signed two weeks after the murders.

Seven others were arrested and charged in the murders. All of them confessed and implicated the others, though all but one have since maintained they are innocent. Dennis Mixon, who admits he was involved in the murders, says Taylor wasn't there.

Taylor's alibi seemed unimpeachable. Shortly after he signed the confession, he recalled that he'd been locked up on a disorderly conduct charge that night. An arrest report showed he was booked at 6:45 p.m. and bonded out at 10 p.m. The murders occurred around 8:45 p.m.

Two weeks after Taylor asserted his alibi, though, two Chicago cops filed a report saying they'd encountered him on the street around 9:30 p.m. that night. Another new witness, a convicted drug dealer and rival gang member, said he'd seen Taylor in Clarendon Park around 7:30 p.m. At trial, prosecutors accused the cops who ran the lockup of shoddy record keeping.

The Confession That Changed Everything

Paperwork, they asserted, isn't foolproof. But confessions are.

By now it's well established that confessions are far from foolproof. Young or mentally impaired suspects are vulner-able to suggestion by investigators. Abuse, torture or prolonged questioning can lead to false confessions.

"Considerable empirical research shows that the potential for false confessions increases markedly when the defendant is a juvenile, placed in isolation and sleep deprived," the appellate decision notes.

Taylor said investigators yelled at him, hit him with a flashlight and told him they'd let him go if he confessed. So he did.

But jurors couldn't get their minds around the notion of a false confession. They found it easier to believe that the cops had messed up the paperwork. "Who knew if he was really in jail?" one told a reporter later.

They might have believed otherwise if they'd seen the evidence that didn't make it to trial. Police reports named a man who was in lockup the night of the murders. Taylor's attorney could have tracked him down -- as Tribune reporters did years later -- to corroborate the alibi. But the defense attorney said he never saw those reports.

The attorney general's office, which is handling the federal appeal, recently came across handwritten notes from interviews with the officers that ran the lockup that night. Those notes could have been used to support Taylor's alibi, but it doesn't appear that they were shared with his lawyers. The attorney general passed them along to Taylor's current attor-ney at Northwestern University's Center on Wrongful Convictions.

So what of that vaunted 2002 reinvestigation? A Tribune review of those documents suggests the exercise focused more on supporting Taylor's conviction than on exploring evidence of his innocence. Investigators didn't interview the cops who worked the lockup the night of the murders or the detectives who obtained the confessions. They were only two-thirds of the way through the investigation when they announced their conclusion that Taylor's conviction was solid.

Like the jurors, they took more stock in Taylor's confession than in the records and witnesses that called it into question.

The federal appellate panel saw things differently. But Taylor, who has spent more than half of his life behind bars, could be years from learning whether he'll get another trial. His attorney, Karen Daniel, has *called for prosecutors to vacate the charges and release him instead -- something we called for back in 2001. At the very least, they ought to drop all roadblocks to a new trial. It's clearer than ever that Taylor didn't get a fair shake the first time.*

Deon's Feedback

As I read through the article, I can't help but feel hopeful. Every word in there feels like another step closer to the truth finally being heard. It's not just about Daniel's case — it's about all of us, everyone who's been stuck in this nightmare for so long. The thought of one of us, Daniel, walking out of this place makes my heart race. I picture it clearly, him stepping into the sunlight, breathing in freedom for the first time in decades. And if that can happen for him, then I know my time is coming too.

That hope is what keeps me going. That belief that justice, no matter how delayed, is still possible. It's been hard to hold onto that sometimes, but moments like this remind me that we're not forgotten. We're closer now than we've ever been.

Chapter 25

A Long-Awaited Freedom

Daniel's Thoughts

2013. That year still feels surreal, like a dream I keep waking up from but never fully leaving behind. My life in prison had become a routine, a monotonous cycle of waiting, hoping, and trying not to lose myself entirely. But on that day, something broke through the fog of my existence, something unexpected and life-changing.

It started like any other day in Menard Correctional Center, a place that felt like it was designed to crush hope. Menard was six hours away from Chicago, and it might as well have been on another planet for how isolated I felt. The guards there had their ways of breaking men, and I had seen enough to know that trust was a luxury I couldn't afford. So when they told me I had an attorney visit, my guard went up. Visits weren't common for me—my family had mostly disappeared after my arrest. My Auntie was the only one who stood by me, God rest her soul. She did what she could, sent money when she could, and visited when she could. But after she passed, those visits stopped.

I was suspicious, to say the least. I thought they were setting me up, maybe to throw me into a cell with some white boys so they could beat the life out of me. I started mentally preparing myself for a fight, layering on extra shirts, sweaters—anything that might soften the blows. But the guards insisted it wasn't a setup. "You actually do have an attorney call," one of them said, but I still didn't believe it. Menard was full of tricks, and this could have been just another one.

The shift commander eventually convinced me that I was safe, or at least safer than I'd thought. I walked to the office, each step feeling like I was walking to my execution. When I picked up the phone, I heard the voice of one of my attorneys, Judith Roy. "Hey Daniel," she said, her voice steady but carrying an undertone that made my stomach twist. "Are you sitting down?"

"No," I replied, not sure why I would need to. "Why do I need to sit?"

"You might want to," she said softly. I didn't sit down, but I gripped the phone tighter.

"Daniel, we're on our way to come get you. They dropped all the charges. You've been exonerated."

I nearly dropped the phone. Exonerated? I had spent so many years dreaming of that word, but now that it was real, it didn't seem possible. Judith explained that Lisa Madigan, the Attorney General, had subpoenaed the police files and found evidence that had been hidden from my defense—evidence that proved my innocence. Reports, interviews, everything that could have cleared my name years ago had been buried, and now it was out in the open.

I should have been happy. I was happy, but there was also a fear that gripped me. What if this was a cruel joke? What if something went wrong, and they didn't release me after all? The emotions were overwhelming—I cried tears of joy, fear, disbelief, and a strange sadness for all the years I'd lost.

I packed up my things quickly, leaving behind everything except my pictures and legal documents. I didn't want to take anything from that place except what mattered. Before I left, I asked the officers if I could see my friend Deon, another man who had been wrongfully imprisoned with me. They took me to him, and when I told him the news, his face fell. "I'm going home, bro," I said, trying to keep my voice steady. "They threw the case out, I'm going home."

Deon looked at me with a mix of happiness and sadness. "I don't want to leave you in here like this," I told him. "We came in together; we should leave together."

He told me not to worry, that he knew if I got out first, the others would follow. And he was right. A few months later, Deon was released too. I was there when he walked out of prison. It was one of the most bittersweet moments of my life—seeing him free but knowing that it came after so much time lost.

When I finally stepped out of Menard, my attorneys, my brother, his girlfriend, and my mom were there to meet me. But even then, the prison tried to hold on. They wanted to keep me in a holding cell until my people arrived. I refused. "If I'm free to go," I told them, "then let me go now." I wasn't going to let them have the last word.

I waited in the parking lot for what felt like hours. When the guards told me I had to leave the property, I felt a rage boil up inside me. They had taken 21 years of my life, and now they wouldn't even let me wait for my family on their property? The audacity of it all was almost too much to bear.

But I was free. For the first time in over two decades, I was free. The world outside those prison walls was both familiar and strange. I didn't know what to expect, but I knew that whatever was waiting for me, it had to be better than what I was leaving behind.

As I sat in the car, driving away from Menard, I felt a mix of relief and an overwhelming sense of loss. How do you reclaim a life that's been stolen? How do you make up for all the moments you'll never get back? I didn't have the answers then, and I'm not sure I have them now. But I knew one thing for certain: I wasn't going to let them take another day from me.

CHICAGO TRIBUNE: 3 Others in Tainted Case Have New Hope
By Steve Mills published Tuesday, July 2, 2013

After man's exoneration in killings, co-defendants seek redress of their own.

The exoneration Friday of a Chicago man convicted of a double murder nearly two decades ago seemed like the end of the story.

It may be only the beginning.

Attorneys for a co-defendant of Daniel Taylor who also has long maintained his innocence filed a petition Monday in Cook Circuit Court seeking his release from prison. They argued that the evidence that unraveled Taylor's conviction—police records showing he was in a lockup when the murders took place in November 1992 – undermines the entire prosecution and should result in freeing Deon Patrick as well.

"We're saying that the confessions were pieced together by the police and have a central fact in each and every one of them that can't be true – because they all have Daniel Taylor spread over all of them," said attorney Stuart Chanen, who represents Patrick. "If they're convinced Taylor was innocent, then Deon Patrick is innocent."

In arresting Taylor, Patrick and six other young men weeks after the murders, Chicago police detectives and Cook County prosecutors pointed to the fact that all eight confessed and implicated each other – strengthening the confessions in the absence of other evidence.

That supposed strength many now prove to be a weakness.

Two of Taylor's other co-defendants said Monday that, like Patrick, they will point to Taylor's release in seeking their own relief in court. Paul Phillips and Lewis Gardner, who eachserved about 15 years in prison for their convictions as supposed lookouts in the murders, told the Tribune they hope to find attorneys to help them overturn their convictions. That would allow them to ask for compensation from the state and file lawsuits against the police seeking big-money damages.

Phillips, who was 17 at the time of his arrest, and Gardner, who was then 15, have also maintained their innocence since their arrests in December 1992.

"Now they know it was all messed up, so it should be clear for myself and Lewis Gardner," said Phillps, who is 37 and has struggled to find work since his release from prison in 2007. "Every job I try to get, they say I've got a felony. No matter how much I try, it doesn't matter. All they do is look at my record."

Taylor was released from prison Friday, hours after prosecutors in Chicago dismissed his conviction. State's Attorney Anita Alvarez later said in a statement that her office would also examine Patrick's conviction and the case of Dennis Mixon.

In a twist of sorts, Mixon has acknowledged he was involved in the double murder and has cleared his seven co-defendants of wrongdoing.

Alvarez's statement made no mention of Phillips or Gardner, but on

A Long-Awaited Freedom

Monday, Sally Daly, a spokeswoman for the office, said prosecutors would "examine each of the cases individually and make the appropriate determination based upon that integrity review." But the cases in which "the defendant is in custody will take priority," she said.

Timothy O'Neill, who teaches criminal procedure at John Marshall Law School, said Taylor's exoneration should help all the co-defendant's but Mixon.

"Certainly it's going to help their argument. It should influence the state's attorney's office and it should influence a judge," said O'Neill, who also writes frequently about issues in criminal law. "There's no magic legal principle, but it destroys the weight of those confessions."

The case stems from the murders of Jeffrey Lassiter and Sharon Haugabook, who were shot in an apartment near Clarendon Park on the city's North Side on Nov. 16, 1992.

Police records showed that Taylor was in the lockup of the old Town Hall police station when the killings took place at 8:45 p.m. He has been arrested at 6:45 p.m. for disorderly conduct and released on bond about 10:00 p.m., according to the records. He was convicted in spite of the records and sentenced to life in prison without parole.

Those police records were crucial to a review by Alvarez's conviction integrity unit and to her decision to set aside Taylor's conviction.

The Tribune first brought the case to light in 2001 in a series of stories investigating false confessions. Since then, the newspaper has uncovered additional evidence that supported Taylor's alibi and, by extension, undermined the convictions of his co-defendants. Taylor's attorneys, Karen Daniel and Judy Royal at the Center on Wrongful Convictions at Northwestern University School of Law, have developed new evidence as well.

Taylor's efforts to prove his innocence gained momentum over the past two years. A federal appeals court declared that it was deeply concerned about the case, saying Taylor's alibi was powerful and his confession questionable. In reviewing the case well, the state attorney general's office then turned over to Taylor's attorneys key documents that bolstered Taylor's alibi but, they asserted, had not been turned over to Taylor's attorneys at trial as required by law.

All of that may prove helpful to Patrick, Phillips and Gardner. In the papers he filed for Patrick on Monday, Chanen urged prosecutors to set *aside Patrick's conviction for two reasons: because he is innocent and because, he argued, prosecutors had withheld key documents.*

Chanen said the documents, though they revolve around Taylor's time in the police lockup, would have helped Patrick as well and should have been turned over by trial prosecutors Thomas Needham and Jeanne Bischoff because they would have helped undermine the entire case.

"They were all entitled to that material, not just Taylor," Chanen said.

Chanen also said the documents supporting Taylor's alibi were corroborated by Mixon's later claims that the other seven young men were not involved as well as two eyewitnesses who said they saw Mixon leave the scene with other men.

Mixon has previously told the Tribune and attorneys the name of one of his alleged accomplices, but he has not revealed the others who took part in the murders. Now 51, Mixon is serving a life sentence at Menard Correctional Center.

"Mixon did a pretty astounding thing," Chanen said. "He literally threw away the jailhouse key."

In the hours before his release Friday from Menard, Taylor sought out Patrick at the prison to say goodbye. He said Patrick began to cry.

Phillips and Gardner said they learned of Taylor's release from one of Taylor's lawyers. The development has raised their hopes. The years since their release have been difficult, they said Monday in phone interviews.

Phillips said he recently landed a job as a baker at a Garrett's popcorn shop at O'Hare International Airport. But then, he said, his conviction was discovered in a background check and he lost the job. It was, he said, one more in a long line of disappointments.

Gardner, who is 34, said he has had jobs in fast food and at a carwash but has struggled too. Living now in Waukegan, he said he has had trouble supporting his girlfriend, their two children and a stepson even though he served his time. He said he does not have the money for a lawyer.

"I thought it was great what happened to Daniel," he said. "Hopefully it can help. I'm praying that it does. I want to get my name cleared and just get a decent job."

Chapter 26

Unshackled Yet Scarred; Life After Injustice

CHICAGO TRIBUNE: *"A Glimmer of Hope: His co-defendant in 2 murders was freed, casting doubt on confessions in the case. Deon Patrick seeks to join his friend." by Steve Mills; July 27, 2013*

MENARD, Ill.- On the day late last month that an exonerated Daniel Taylor walked out of the state prison here, Deon Patrick held an emotional farewell meeting with his close friend, expressing hope that he, too, would be freed soon.

After all, both were sentenced to life in prison without the possibility of parole for a 1992 double murder. The cases against them and six co-defendants were built on confessions in which all eight incriminated each other.

Patrick and his lawyers believe that the fatal flaw in Taylor's case – that he was being held in a police station lockup when the murders took place – would unravel Patrick's conviction as well since the cases were so tightly intertwined through the interlocking confessions.

In a lengthy interview this week at Menard C0rrectional Center in southern Illinois, Patrick struck a bittersweet note, elated for his friend but frustrated that he remains locked up.

"It was hard to watch him leave," Patrick, 41, who has been imprisoned for about half his life. "But by the same token I wanted this to happen because it meant finally somebody was listening."

Patrick finds himself in the same position as other inmates whose co-defendants had been exonerated – left behind but not without hope.

After death row inmate Aaron Patterson was pardoned by then-Gov. George Ryan in 2003, co-defendant Eric Caine waited eight years until his release, even though both cases were built on confessions obtained by the police through torture. Just this week the Chicago City Council approved a payout of $10 million to Cain to settle his wrongful-conviction lawsuit.

Herbery Whitlock was released in 2008, four years after co-defendant Gordon "Randy" Steidl was set free, despite the fact that the evidence against both in a 1986 double murder in Edgar County in east central Illinois depended on witnesses whose testimony had been undermined.

For Patirck, much like in thoses cases, the lion's share of attention had long been directed at Taylor, whose alibi that he was in custody at the time of the murders was unusual and powerful.

After Taylor's release June 28, Cook County State's Attorney Anita Alvarez said her office began an in-depth review of Patrick's conviction and vowed to work with urgency since Patrick remains in prison.

Alvarez's words are cold comfort for Patrick, though. He said he had watched with dismay as prosecutors fought for close to two decades to keep Taylor in prison, despite police records showing he was locked up when the murders occurred.

"It sometimes makes you wonder how they do the things they do and then go to sleep at night," Patrick said in a small prison room separated by glass from a reporter.

Patrick is a thick-set man with gray creeping into his neatly trimmed beard. He has a deep voice, and his dark eyes sometimes give him an almost baleful expression. But that is belied by the easy smile that frequently breaks out across his face and his warm manner.

Patrick recalled how after the death of his mother when he was 16 he spent a lot of time on the street, at one point picking up a robbery conviction that sent him to a boot camp for four months.

"It changed the course of my life," he said of her death. "It made me have to become grown when I wasn't ready for it."

Patrick was 20 when he was arrested with Taylor and six others for the fatal shootings of Jeffrey Lassiter and Sharon Haugabook in Lassiter's apartment, not far from Clarendon Park on Chicgo's North Side.

Patrick said he asked police to call a lawyer who had represented him on another case but they refused. He said the detectives and a prosecutor, Assistant State's Attorney Joe Magats, pressed him to admit his role in the murders but that he repeatedly refused.

"I'm telling them I didn't know nothing about the crime," he said.

Patrick said the detectives showed him statements from some of his co-defendants implicating him in the murders and even brought some of them into the interrogation room and told him they had identified him as being involved in the crime. Still, Patrick said, he started to lose all hope of ever being released and signed a four-page confession that Magats wrote out for him.

"It was a mental strain, the threats of never seeing your kids again, the threats of going to death row," Patrick said.

"Magats, who also took Taylor's longer formal confession, now is a deputy chief of the criminal prosecutions bureau, a high-ranking post in the state's attorney's office. He declined to comment for this story through an office spokeswoman,

In the confession, Patrick identified himself as a member of the Conservative Vice Lords street gang since he was about 9 and said that he, Taylor and two others went inside Lassiter's apartment while four other teens stayed outside and acted as lookouts. According to Patrick's confession, co-defendant Dennis Mixon gave him a gun and Patrick shot Lassiter. Mixon then shot Haugabook, the confession said.

Taylor's confession, though, claimed that Patrick shot both victims.

"The sole piece of evidence against Deon was his confession. There wasn't any physical evidence. And nothing else," said Nicole Auerbach, Patrick's attorney. "And what we know now is that this couldn't possibly have happened the way they said it happened."

Patrick said he could not offer police an alibi after his arrest two weeks following the murders because he could not recall where he was that night. Later, though, he said he remembered he had been at the home of a friend's sister watching a football game on TV.

At Patirck's trial, his attorney did not call the friend's sister as a witness to support his alibi, and Patrick did not testify in his own defense. Years later, the woman provided Patrick an affidavit confirming his alibi.

Patrick was convicted by a jury. Prosecutors sought the death penalty, but he was sentenced to life in prison.

Three of the co-defendants either had their charges thrown out or were acquitted at trial, but Taylor, Mixon and two others were convicted with Patrick. The two others received shorter sentences and are free. But Mixon, who is serving a life sentence, has since admitted taking part in the murders and absolved the other seven of involvement. Je has even named another man as an accomplice in the killings.

Prison, according to Patrick, has been "miserable." He missed his two young children growing up and has had few visits from his family or friends. His hopes were raised when a 2001 Tribune investigation, while focusing largely on Taylor and uncovering additional evidence of his innocence, suggested that the entire case was flawed. But prosecutors continued to fight.

Patrick's hopes were raised again when Alvarez's predecessor, Dick Devine, launched an investigation into the prosecution in response to stories in the Tribune.

But Patrick said officials from the office tried to get him to implicate another man in the murders and showed no interest in his claim of innocence. Documents that were later turned over to Taylor's attorneys suggested Devine's inquiry was focused on preserving the convictions.

"It was almost like we were back at the police station," Patrick said of the officials who talked with him at the time. "They were yelling."

Now, Patrick has a new found hope. After Taylor's goodbye, he said he turned off his TV and began studying his case again. By chance, that same day he received in the mail a copy of a new appeal that his lawyers were filing. What's more, he learned that Alvarez's conviction integrity unit would review his case after throwing out Taylor's conviction. He was reluctant to be optimistic, he said, but hope crept in anyway.

He has begun to let himself daydream about seeing his children – now adults – in the outside world. He has also let himself think of seeing Taylor again.

"I know that one day I'll be able to be out there with him," Patrick said.

Unshackled Yet Scarred; Life After Injustice

Deon's Thoughts

Two decades; 21 Years, one month and eight days to be exact. That's how long I had been locked away, trapped in a nightmare for a crime I didn't commit. Twenty years of my life, lost to the unforgiving bars and cold concrete of a prison cell. It was Christmas 2013, and the thought of spending another birthday in that place was like a weight pressing down on my chest. My family had always believed that I'd be home for the holidays that year. They held onto that hope with a fierceness that both lifted and crushed me. But as the days ticked by and the legal battles dragged on, even their hope began to wane.

Then, late in December, I got a letter from my attorney. The state had challenged the latest petition, pushing my next court date to February 2014. It was like a punch to the gut, another cruel delay in a process that had already drained so much from me. I felt myself slipping into despair, thinking I'd have to endure more waiting, more heartache. But then, out of nowhere, a phone call changed everything.

It was January 9th, 2014. My attorney Nicole got a call from the State's Attorney's Office. They asked if she could be in court the next morning. When she and my other attorney Stuart arrived, they were met by the state's attorney, who handed them a piece of paper. Nicole's hands trembled as she read the words: "We vacate his conviction today. Go pick him up as soon as we leave the courtroom."

But I knew nothing of this. That morning, in the cold, dark confines of my cell, the routine was abruptly interrupted. The guards came and fired me from my kitchen job, moving me out of my cell without a word of explanation. I was confused, on edge. I had seen it happen before—men told they were going home, only to have that promise yanked away in a cruel twist of fate. I braced myself for the worst, for another disappointment.

Then, as I stood by the gate, a guard I recognized from years in the facility came up to me with a grin. "Pack your stuff and go home," he said, his tone light, almost teasing. I froze, unable to process the words. Was this another cruel joke? Was I still trapped in the nightmare that had been my life for the past 20 years?

But he wasn't joking. "You're going home," he repeated, and slowly, the reality began to sink in. I gathered my belongings—the few possessions I had accumulated over the years: a TV, a radio, some food. I gave them away to the friends who had shared my fate for so long. I wouldn't need any of it anymore. Then, with a mix of disbelief and cautious hope, I stepped into the shower, letting the water wash over me, trying to absorb the fact that this time, it was real.

By the time I was led out of the cellblock, the sky had darkened. It was almost 9 PM by the time my family—who had driven seven long hours from Chicago—arrived to pick me up. The first faces I saw were my son, Daniel, and Nicole. My son, now a grown man, had struggled to believe the news. After years of broken promises and shattered hopes, he was afraid that this too would be taken away. But when he saw me, walking free for the first time in over two decades, he finally allowed himself to believe.

The hug we shared in front of the penitentiary was the first in 21 years. I had last held him when he was just 11 months old. Now, standing before me was a young man, tears streaming down his face, as we embraced. There were no words to capture the depth of that moment—the mixture of joy, relief, and lingering disbelief.

I wasn't sure the reality of my freedom had fully set in as we made the drive back. I sat in the car, the world outside a blur, my mind struggling to catch up with this new reality. When we stopped at a restaurant near the prison, it felt like a strange new world. I hadn't been in a restaurant in over two decades, and everything seemed foreign. The other diners seemed too loud, too close, their behavior unsettling in ways I couldn't quite articulate. The sight of unfamiliar foods like crawfish—things I had never had the chance to try—overwhelmed me. I stuck to a simple burger and fries, not too anxious to venture into the unknown just yet.

Finally, we arrived at my cousin's house in Country Club Hills, a far cry from the West Side of Chicago where I had grown up. The block was dark, but my cousin's house was alive with light and warmth. Inside, nearly 30 people were waiting for me—cousins, aunts, uncles, and friends, all gathered to welcome me home. It was 3 AM, but no one cared about the hour. The room was filled with laughter, tears, and stories—stories of the years that had been lost, but also stories of hope and the future that now stretched before me.

As the night turned into morning, I finally allowed myself to breathe. For the first time in 21 years, I wasn't in a cell, surrounded by bars and concrete. I was with my family, my real family, in a place that felt like home. But even as I lay down to rest, sleep didn't come easily. The weight of my past was still there, heavy and unyielding, and the future—though bright—was uncertain.

The next day was a blur of activity. More family and friends came by, eager to see me, to hug me, to share in my newfound freedom. I found myself caught between the joy of being home and the harsh reality that life outside wasn't going to be easy. I needed to find a job, a place to live, and, perhaps hardest of all, I needed to rebuild the relationships that had been fractured by my long absence.

The reunion with my old friend who had been released in 1995, was particularly bittersweet. He had offered me a place to stay, but I, still reeling from years of abandonment, couldn't accept. The years had changed us both, and I wasn't the same man I had been when we first met. I had been hardened by the years, shaped by the struggles I had faced alone, and I wasn't ready to let old wounds reopen.

Instead, I focused on my family, especially my children. The years apart had left deep scars, and now, with my newfound freedom, I was determined to heal them. But it was harder than I had imagined. My children were no longer kids; they were adults, with lives and struggles of their own. They had grown up without me, and the bond we should have shared was fragile, strained by the years of separation.

My return had brought hope, but it also brought new challenges. I was a free man, but freedom came with its own set of obstacles. I had to navigate a world that had moved on without me, reconnect with a family that had learned to live without me, and find my place in a society that still saw me as the man I had been, not the man I had become.

As the days turned into weeks, I began to adjust to my new life. I found a job, secured a place to live, and slowly, tentatively, began to rebuild my relationship with my children. But the road ahead was long, and the scars of the past wouldn't heal overnight.

My first year of freedom was a journey of discovery—of who I was, who I had become, and who I wanted to be. It was a year of challenges, but also a year of hope, a year of new beginnings. And as I looked to the future, I knew that while the past would always be a part of me, it didn't have to define me. I was free, truly free, for the first time in over 20 years. And that, I knew, was just the beginning.

CHICAGO TRIBUNE "Cleared of double murder after 21 years, man sues city" by Brian Slodysko; May 20, 2014

Deon Patrick says he was "no angel" when cops took him to a North Side lockup in 1992, cuffed him to a wall and –over the course of 28 hours – talked him into a double-murder confession.

But Patrick, who served 21 years in prison before murder charges against him were dropped, never made "the leap from selling dime bags to double murder," Stuart Chanen, one of Patrick's attorneys, said Monday.

And now, equipped with a certificate of innocence exonerating him of the 1992 slaying of Jeffrey Lassiter and Sharon Haugabook, Patrick says it's time for those who put him in prison to pay.

Standing before an array of TV cameras in a downtown law office, Patrick and his lawyers announced a 13-count federal lawsuit against the city of Chicago and the Cook County state's attorney's office. The suit also names Chicago police detectives who worked on the Uptown case, as well as prosecutors who argued for his conviction. The suit does not specify the amount of compensation being sought.

"I want the people that put me there intentionally to experience everything I've experienced," said Patrick, 42, who was released from the Menard Correctional Center in January. "But that's not going to happen. So the only form of justice I see is filing the civil suit."

The suit claims the police detective railroaded Patrick and five other young men, ages 15 to 22, by coercing them to turn on each other during the lengthy interrogations. One by one, the detainees signed statements falsely implicating themselves and each other, Patrick said.

"We tried to talk ourselves out of trouble. In this case we talked ourselves into trouble," Patrick said.

Patrick's co-defendant, Daniel Taylor, already has filed a civil rights suit against the city; the suit is pending in federal court. Taylor, who served 20 years, was instrumental in the case against the men falling apart –

albeit years after their convictions and with the help of Northwestern University Innocence Project.

Taylor's attorney's argued he couldn't have committed the murders because he was in police custody, locked up on a disorderly conduct charge at the time.

Chanen and Patrick's other lawyer, Nicol Auerbach, said the actions of the detectives who worked the case fit a troubling pattern that says a lot about the police department culture of the 1990s.

"The Chicago Police Department...engaged in a pattern of unlawfully coercing confessions over a period of years, frequently preying on young African-American men in order to close unsolved cases through overzealous methods of interrogation," the suit claims.

Patrick, who was 20 when he was charged, said he was a member of the Vice Lords gang and had been arrested about 20 times. He was well-known on his block when police scooped him up as a murder suspect. But the night of the murder he had been at a friend's house – a fact that played a role in his release, Chanen said.

Patrick, who has returned to his family and now-grown children in Hazel Crest, offered some advice to others who find themselves in similar circumstances.

"Always request your attorney to be present," Patrick said.

Deon Continues

After coming home, within the first couple of weeks, I was on the docket with the Cook County State's Attorney's Office to receive my Certificate of Innocence (COI), which they granted without contest. Having this paper proved that they truly believed I was innocent because they vacated my conviction and gave me a COI. But over the next few months, the civil phase started, and during this time, I felt like I was going through it all over again. It felt like 1992 again with deposition after deposition. This process dragged on for months, with negotiations over what evidence would be allowed in the trial. What I learned was that they were doing their best to keep out any evidence that could help me and prove my innocence. It felt like they didn't even want my

COI to matter. They didn't want certain people, like Karen Daniel, to testify about how they proved we were innocent.

A few months later, we got a trial date, and that's when reality hit. They weren't giving up, and they weren't going to admit they were wrong. To this day, they have never admitted they were wrong and that we shouldn't have been there in the first place. So, when the trial began, it felt like I was on trial for my life all over again, even though I wasn't the defendant this time. The arresting officers and the State's Attorney's office were the defendants, but their lawyers put on a case that tried to imply that we had committed this murder and that they had just let us go. This was impossible because all of our evidence proved we didn't do it and that we shouldn't have been there from the beginning. Yet, they still wouldn't take ownership of what they did to us and let us feel fully vindicated.

The trial was supposed to last six to eight weeks, but it was filled with a lot of idle conversation. They claimed to have 10,000 pieces of evidence proving I was guilty, but they didn't have one. They read fabricated police reports, autopsy reports, and every document ever filed in my case for six to eight weeks, calling it their "evidence." All of it had already fallen apart years ago when we proved we couldn't have committed the crime. To me, the trial was a waste of taxpayer money and everyone's time. One thing I learned is that the system is set up in a way that lawyers defending these officers and the State's Attorney's office file frivolous motions just to rack up billable hours and make money. They defend people they know are guilty just to get paid, and they walk away with millions of dollars from the state.

In the end, the jury ruled in my favor, and it was a sigh of relief. But even then, it wasn't over. It still took another four, almost five, years for the case to fully end. Only then was I able to move my family and start a new life in peace. Yet, even with that, it feels like we're still looking for full closure, trying to write the last chapter of this story. Now, at least, we can tell our story the way it truly happened without being challenged by people fabricating evidence.

The civil case gave us some sense of closure, but I don't think anyone who's been through something like this will ever fully close the door on what happened. It takes so much out of you, and you keep thinking about it, bringing up all kinds of emotions. Having to sit in front of them and be attacked all over again takes you back to when you were just a scared kid sitting in an interrogation room, dealing with seasoned people who knew how to break you. But by the time of the trial, I was 43 or 44 years old. I wasn't that scared kid anymore. I was a grown man, and I knew they couldn't harm me because there were too many witnesses around.

Going through that trial, being able to speak my truth, and getting it out in front of the jury was powerful for me. It helped me, and it allowed them to understand what really happened to me. In the end, my civil case turned out in my favor. My family and I are doing well now, and we've moved away from that kind of scrutiny. I was able to get everything expunged and sealed, so if I get pulled over, none of that stuff comes up in my name anymore. My life is much better now, and I'm just trying to write my own story. I'm not letting what happened to me dictate my life anymore. Moving forward, I want to write my own legacy and show the world who I really am.

Daniel's Thoughts

I remember Joseph Brown, or "Slick" as we called him on the streets, had beaten the case during the motions and tasted freedom, even if it was just for a little while. He passed away in 2011, and when I heard the news, it hit me hard. It was like another heavy blow on top of everything I was already carrying. What really got to me was knowing Joseph never even found out that the rest of us had been exonerated; he died without knowing we were still fighting in his name.

Lewis' Thoughts

I initially never wanted to pursue a civil lawsuit against the state. The thought of going through all of that again—reliving the nightmare—was too much to bear. When the lawyers contacted me, I was hesitant. I didn't want their money. No amount of money could give me back the life I lost. All I wanted was to be left alone, to live my life in peace.

Now, years later, life is better. I have my ups and downs, but I'm here. I'm alive, and I'm with the people I love. My wife and I bought a house, and we're raising our kids. I still have my moments where the past comes back to haunt me, but I'm learning to move forward. I'm learning to live again.

And that's all I ever wanted—to live, to be free. And I'm finally getting there.

Paul's Thoughts

Amen, I just want to give praise and thanks to God for everything he has done in my life.
One thing I know is that when you have things harboring in your life or things that you'll be holding on inside of you, you have to release it and let it go.
See God, don't want us to hold on to anything.
But I know we are human. I know we try to let everything go, but we still hold on to it.
I know things get really hard in our lives and I want to thank God for removing everything I've been holding on to, and everything I need to release.
Me, releasing.
Sit in the backseat of a car. I didn't tremble,
I didn't even get read my rights. I didn't even see a memo.
Stuck in the limbo. I tried to keep everything so simple,
but when I look back, all I see is my mom staring out the window.
I guess that's the last time I see a familiar face,
hoping God has his hand on me, save me by His grace.
That left me with an awkward taste
in an awkward space
where you know the first years of your life have been erased.
It's not safe to run a race that you can't escape,
knowing it was a setup all along, but now they are saying it was a mistake.
It's too late, because even when I'm asleep, I'm awake
and in pain in my heart all it did was make my heart beat ache.
All I wanted was my freedom.

Unshackled Yet Scarred; Life After Injustice

And even though I went in front of a judge, I sure thought I would beat him.
I'm hoping the judge would read them and see right through him and read them.
And even with tears in my eyes, doesn't mean I couldn't see him.
I'm seeing the cops deceive him and the judge is going to believe him.
I'm hearing the words guilty,
but I was looking for the word free him, and the people in the courtroom saying,
oh, I hate to be him.
And I asked the judge, can I see my family? I couldn't see him.
Do y'all believe that the judge would even let me see my family?
After 15 years. I still need answers.
My mom was still struggling, but my dad was dying from cancer,
and my twins, I thought I would see I didn't even have the chance to,
because as soon as my dad passed away, my twins died right after
It was another end to a sad chapter. But all I can hear in my head are the voices of the police, laughter and the rage is overshadowing and my heart beat faster
and I want to attack but God said. You cannot serve two masters.
So, what should I do? Should I give everything up God and continue to follow you,
YES, MY SON but that's what I must continue to do,
because I'm doing it all for God.

One night, I was out, just trying to forget everything, when something changed. I don't know if it was the sunrise or just exhaustion, but I felt like God was telling me I couldn't keep living like that. That's when I decided I needed to clear my name, to finally put all this behind me for good. I started reaching out to lawyers, but most of them said my case was too risky, too complicated. It felt like I was hitting the same wall over and over again.

But then in 2014, things started to change. I don't remember all the details, but I know it had something to do with Daniel getting released. Once that happened, things started to fall into place. We got the People's Law Office involved, and eventually, I got a call saying I was being

The Hazel Boyz

granted a Certificate of Innocence. I was at my stepmom's place in Oak Park, down in the basement, when I got the news. I just sat there, in shock, and then I started praying, thanking God for finally hearing me. But even with that certificate, life didn't magically get easier. My record still popped up sometimes. I remember getting pulled over in Texas, and the cops saw my old charges. They questioned me like I was still a criminal, and I had to explain over and over that I was innocent. It was frustrating, to say the least.

It's wild how life comes full circle in ways you can't even imagine. Back in the '80s, when I was just a kid, I had a run-in with a cop that I thought would be just another painful memory. He drove over me with his police truck with no hesitation. I didn't know who he was then, just another part of the system that was always working against us, pushing us down. I tried to leave that moment behind as life moved forward, but as fate would have it, I couldn't. Years later, when I was caught up in the court system, I discovered he wasn't a cop anymore—no, he'd moved up. He became a lawyer.

It hit me like a punch to the gut. My legal team didn't realize who he was at first, but over time, as we pieced everything together, the picture became clearer. He was the same person who'd injured me as a child. How does that even happen? How does someone like that get to decide what happens to people, to me? It makes you question everything—how much of the system was rigged from the start. This man was supposed to uphold the law, yet he was the very person who caused me harm and now sits in a position of power. To make matters worse, the incident report from when I was run over has disappeared without a trace. When it came time for me to access the money I had won from the lawsuit, I wasn't able to receive it until I turned 18. But by the time I turned 18, the lawyers had taken the money.

When my lawyers began to uncover the layers of this mess, they tried to reach out to him. They wanted to confront him, to get him to acknowledge what he'd done. But, just like before, he refused to cooperate. He didn't want to help, didn't want to face the truth of what he'd done—not to me, not to my family, not to anyone.

And now, he's a judge. How does someone like that get to be in charge of justice? It's hard not to feel bitter about it, to wonder if the cards were stacked against us from the very beginning. But you know what? Despite all that, I'm still here. I survived. And though it still hurts, though the weight of that memory still lingers, I didn't let him win—not then, and not now.

Today, life is better, but it's still a struggle. I started a trucking company in South Carolina, trying to build something for myself. My brother and his wife are into gospel music, and I've been helping out with that too. Music has always been a part of my life, a way to cope, to express what I can't always put into words. But no matter what I do, that past is always there, like a scar that doesn't fully heal. Some days are good, some not so much, but I keep moving forward. I have to. Because after everything, I've learned that giving up isn't an option.

Daniel's Thoughts

At this stage in life, I can honestly say I've found peace, clarity, and a renewed sense of purpose. I'm blessed with a supportive community around me, filled with people who not only want to see me succeed but also help keep me grounded. Through the experiences of others, I've realized that not every lesson has to be learned firsthand; sometimes, we can avoid unnecessary hardship simply by observing and listening to those who've walked the path before us.

After everything I've endured, especially during my wrongful imprisonment, I've come to appreciate the importance of both emotional and mental freedom. Physically, I've been free for 11 years now—June 28th marked that milestone—but not mentally free, the shedding of institutionalized habits and thoughts, is something that I continue to work on daily. I consciously reflect before reacting to ensure that I'm not carrying over any negative traits from my past. It's an ongoing journey, but one I'm committed to, especially for my son.

My son who is nine years old is my greatest inspiration. Everything I do, every decision I make, is with him in mind. I want to give him the love and guidance that I longed for in my own life. Every time I pick him up from school and see him run into my arms, I'm reminded of how blessed I am to be here for him and provide the support and love that every child deserves.

The Hazel Boyz

I'm grateful to Allah for every experience, every hardship, and every joy. People often ask if I would change the 21 years I spent in prison, and the answer is no. Those years shaped me, molded me, and brought me to where I am today. I've prayed for life, and with that comes everything—the good and the bad. I embrace it all because I know it's part of the journey.

I also want to give a special shout-out to my brothers from that time—Lewis, Deon, Paul, Joseph, Akia, and Rodney. We've been through so much together, and I want you to know that my love and respect for each of you runs deep. No matter what, we'll always have each other. If you ever need to talk, I'm just a call away. We may have been in different places physically, but spiritually, we were always together. You are my brothers for life.

Lastly, I want the world to know that despite the challenges, the pain, and the injustices, I'm not bitter. I'm happy, I'm free, and I'm grateful. This journey is far from over, and I plan to continue living it with love, positivity, and purpose.

Chapter 27

Healing Through Words

The weight of what happened still lingers with them sometimes. The pain resurfaces, especially in quiet moments of reflection, even though everyone tells them it's okay. They carry it still, unable to fully release it, as if their hearts refuse to accept the words they keep repeating to themselves: *"It's not your fault."* They've said it so many times, trying to lift the burden off their shoulders, but somehow, it never fully goes away.

And maybe it's because they were just kids—young, impressionable, and vulnerable—preyed upon by a system that cared more about closing a case than finding the truth. *"We didn't do this,"* they'd tell each other, reminding themselves of their innocence. *"You didn't start this. They did this to us."* Every time they spoke, there was nothing but love and reassurance between them, a bond that couldn't be shattered.

That bond, forged in the fires of their shared suffering, had been there before the nightmare began and had only grown stronger through the years. *"I loved you then, and I love you even more now,"* Daniel had told them, a testament to how much their brotherhood meant. The false accusations, the years of wrongful imprisonment, the agony—they hadn't broken the connection between them. Instead, they had fortified it.

Now, they knew it was time to let their hearts heal, to release the weight they had been carrying for far too long. They understood that the pain would never truly disappear—that deep ache for the lost years and the lives they could never reclaim would remain. But they had fought so hard, not just for their own freedom, but for each other's. That fight was their shared triumph, a testament to their resilience.

Freedom from the physical bars was one thing, but being free from the mental and emotional chains was another. They wanted to live—really live—without the constant pain hanging over them like a shadow. They had won their lawsuit against the state, but freedom didn't mean that everything was magically okay. There were still scars, still wounds that hadn't fully healed. But they had each other, and with that, they knew they could make it through.

They remembered the days when they felt alone, burdened with the full weight of their situation. But now, that weight was lighter because they had fought together. They were determined to move forward, not just as survivors but as men stronger than ever before. *"This is what life means to me—these moments with us. I want more of these moments,"* Daniel had said, and they all agreed.

It was time to live. Truly live. And they would do it together.

Chapter 28

Resources

People's Law Office
　1180 N. Milwaukee Ave., Chicago, IL 60642
　Tel.: 773-235-0070 | Fax: 773-235-6699
　https://peopleslawoffice.com/

Center on Wrongful Convictions: Northwestern Pritzker School of Law
　375 East Chicago Avenue, Chicago IL 60611-3069
　Phone: 312-503-2391| Fax: 312-503-8977
　Email: cwc@law.northwestern.edu
　https://cwc.law.northwestern.edu/

Books
　True Stories of False Confessions Edited by Rob Warden and Steven A Drizin
　The Black's Law Dictionary by Author: Bryan A. Garner
　Acts Of Faith: Daily Meditations for People of Colour by Iyanla Vanzant

Credible Sources:

In *The Hazel Boyz: The Trials of Four Innocent Men*, factual details about the wrongful convictions and legal battles of Daniel Taylor and his co-defendants are drawn from an archival article published by the *Chicago Tribune*. For further reference, see:

Ezorn, Eric Zorn. "Tribune Archive: The Daniel Taylor Case." *Chicago Tribune*, February 2013. Available at: https://blogs.chicagotribune.com/news_columnists_ezorn/2013/02/tribune-archive-the-daniel-taylor-case.html.

Court Documents

City of Chicago Detective Divisions Area 3 Violent Crimes, Complaint Register No. 197331. (1992). Filed in the Circuit Court of Cook County, Illinois.

City of Chicago Detective Divisions, Area 3 Violent Crimes, Homicide/Murder Case File for Jeffrey Lassiter, RD# T-543-021, March 3, 1993.

All sources provided critical insight into the case, highlighting the systemic failures within the justice system that played a significant role in the wrongful convictions explored in this book.